THE RIVER

Best wishes, Cindy!

Kelwyn

ISBN: 978-0-615-63962-8

For Eurith, lovely and loving

ACKNOWLEDGMENTS

During my time I've learned much about life and fishing from many friends and relatives. My father, Floyd Ellis, the Stricklen uncles—Fate, Robert, Frank, and George, Babe Chessir, Cousin Carl Dellinger and A.V. Bruce, Larry Landreth, David Day, nephew Eddie Ervin, Eurith's dad Earl and her cousin Richard Ervin, Charlie Coder, Garlan Tayler, stepbrother Winfred Alexander. Thanks to you all.

I've a special thanks to my daughter, Sherri, who put this together, edited it and provided constant encouragement. And to Eurith for all she did for my life.

PROLOGUE

When I was a young man, my dad, my mother's brothers and I fished the, then, pristine waters of Glover, Mountain Fork, the Cossatot, and the Saline. These rivers had many delightful fish-loaded tributaries which were cold, clear, clean and utterly drinkable. The dense forests also held an amazing variety of wildlife. We often saw, and sometimes, had to deal with, razorback hogs, deer, raccoons, possums, an occasional bobcat, and, once in a while, a rattlesnake (though not often because the hogs kept them under control.) My Uncle Fate and I once surprised a couple of black bear enjoying the crop from blackberry vines that had grown up along a tramway long since abandoned by the Dierks Lumber Company. The two of them, probably a mother and cub, just grunted and moved to the other side of the bushes. Uncle Fate and I just grunted and moved in the other direction, FAST!

Once, when camped at the Arsenic cave on the Saline, long after we'd all gone to sleep, a cougar woke us up with a blood-curdling cry under the campground bluff. The next morning several of us walked down the steep pathway to the river. There, at the water's edge, in a sandy area, were the pug marks of a **big** cat!

The forest itself was a complex mix of pines and hardwoods. Many of the hardwoods were nut and acorn producers. Squirrels were abundant and were often harvested for a mess of fried squirrel and dumplings. Bends in the river with deeper, accumulated topsoil, often had a growth of mulberry trees and were an excellent spot for a stealthy hunter to get one or two squirrels for the pot before beginning the day's fly-fishing.

We thoroughly explored these streams and forests over a span of years from the 1930s until the mid-1960s. We never saw Sasquatch, his tracks, or his friends!

The amazing bio-diversity of the forest depends upon the willingness of man to practice common sense with respect to factors such as waste disposal and development which influences the integrity of the river systems.

As the river runs to the sea it gives rise to coastal marshes and estuaries. The organisms that inhabit these near-shore and in-shore areas require the river's flow as a source of nutrients and fresh-water. Without the modifying effects of this water, many of the estuaries become hyper-saline and incapable of consistently supporting many of the organisms which are important biologically and economically to us. Thus, long-term droughts often reduce the yield of oysters, crabs and shrimp. These same estuaries provide a place of refuge and nutrition for the larval stages of many of our sport-fish. Redfish, sea trout, mullet, drum, flounder and many others depend upon healthy estuaries for successful completion of their life cycles.

Pollution of rivers, marshes and estuaries can be even more disastrous in the long term than droughts as a result of the toxicity of pesticides, herbicides, and heavy metals involved in industrial processes. Much of these poisonous substances gradually become incorporated into the estuary mud and, even after remedial procedures have reduced their concentration in the bay's waters, toxicity levels may increase to a severely harmful point during floods and hurricanes and other bottom-disturbing processes. As a result of the happenings, a number of bays along the Texas coast have been declared off-limits to harvests of shell-fish and have posted warnings against consumption of fin-fish and fish-kills often occur.

Bay systems and estuaries are environmentally fragile—the river is their life blood, just as is the case of our forests. Clean, productive river systems will maintain a clean, productive sea coast.

PART 1: RED RIVER

1 INTRODUCTION

Red River is a broad, murky, flat-land stream originating in eastern New Mexico. It drains a tremendous area of Oklahoma, Texas, and Louisiana. Its pathway is a meandering one, through its lush, fertile valley to its junction with the Atchafalaya River near Simmesport, Louisiana.

The lower reaches of the river are especially rich as a result of silt deposition in the flood plain during overflow times. This topsoil is many feet thick in some areas and has long been an important producer of alfalfa, corn, cotton and other agricultural crops.

In some areas there has been extensive depletion of the top- soil and subsequent loss of productivity. The culprit is probably a combination of erosion by wind and water, failure to plant soil-building crops and excessive use of pesticides and herbicides which may tend to eliminate soil-building micro-organisms. As a result of flowing through such a fertile environment the river has been extremely productive as a fishery and so have its oxbow lakes, cut-offs, and sloughs.

In centuries past, the surroundings consisted of dense forests and isolated, open areas or meadows. Commercially important varieties of timber were plentiful, as were many types of game animals.

A Denison Herald Frontier Times article for July 1876 made note of the establishment of a sawmill venture on the north shore of Eagle Lake, one of the large oxbows, in what was then Indian Territory, and, later, Oklahoma. According to the article, the bottom-land surrounding the lake was a rich source of oak, bois d'arc, and walnut sufficient for supporting the sawmill industry for many years. In addition, the lake was capable of becoming an important commercial fishery for a variety of species. There was also an abundance of game animals.in the forest: including bear, squirrels, quail, and deer. Predators encountered were wolves, bobcats, coyotes, and cougars. In season, ducks and geese were enormously plentiful.

Time and men took their toll on the river and lakes. Most of the bottomland forest was gone by the late 1930's. An exception was a rather large forest remnant on the east side of Eagle Lake and extending a mile or more back to the river. This was a dense, heavily timbered area that persisted until the early 1960's.

In spite of the changes that have occurred during the past 70 years this area had maintained its productivity of fish and game up until the past decade. However, continued heavy use of pesticides and herbicides, along with pollution from dairies and gravel pits have hastened deterioration of this once beautiful, productive area almost to a point of no return.

In this little book my intent is to share many of the experiences I've enjoyed during the past half century on the river, its tributaries and its lakes. This is how I remember it.

2 BROWN'S CREEK

Some years the mouth of Brown's Creek drained directly into the river. If the meandering of the main channel took Red River farther toward the Texas bank, the creek drained into a backwater slough which had become a snag-filled lake of several acres.

Either situation was good for fishing. The back water lake was full of fish. The most numerous, of course, were gar, buffalo, and carp, but some years it was also loaded with crappie and a smattering of black bass. At these times a bucket of shiners could yield heavy stringers of good eating fish. One spring, Eurith's (my wife) Uncle Lee caught a seven pound largemouth bass around one of the snags, while crappie fishing!

This lake was shallow, about four or five feet maximum. A person studying animal tracks in the soft mud around it could find evidence of coons, possums, bobcats and, rarely, deer.

The high banks along the river bed were heavily forested with a variety of oaks, cottonwoods, and pecans. There were usually lots of squirrels, and hunters frequently got their limits. But, one had to hunt with an eye to the ground since cottonmouths were common though not abundant. One of the Chessir boys killed a rattlesnake measuring over five feet long while squirrel hunting near the mouth of the creek.

At least three kinds of wild grapes were common in these woods. They included tiny, but delicious, possum grapes, larger summer grapes which began ripening in late July, and mustang grapes which ripened usually in September. Eurith and I picked these wild fruits for making the world's best jelly every year from the mid 1960's until around 1980, when new landowners raised new fences with gates and locks, denying access to this area of the river.

In the years in which the main river channel was at the Oklahoma bank, the creek opened up directly into the current. Fishing was, at times, excellent. Almost any kind of bait worked: live minnows, crawfish, worms, stink bait, cut bait, and would usually bring in a good mixed bag of blue cat, channels, and drum. After a summer rainstorm, while the creek was pouring fresh, muddy water into the river, baiting with red worms could account for some surprising catches. I recall one such time in which, by casting a worm-baited hook into the rough water, I was able to string up a couple of dozen small channel cats of around 3/4 of a pound to 1 pounds. Mixed in with the catfish were nice-sized drum up to a couple of pounds and several shovel-nosed sturgeon. One day, under such conditions, I caught eighteen of these strange looking fish. The largest was about three pounds. During those years I caught lots of sturgeon but only after a rain and in muddy, fresh water.

During low water periods, the creek would clear up nicely. Caving banks usually made for an abundance of brush piles and, with worms, small shiners, or grasshoppers it was possible to catch a nice mess of hand-sized crappie and thick bodied beautifully colored bream, many of which were larger than the average creek crappie.

Brown's Creek was the main tributary of Red River for the area including the communities of Yarnaby and Yuba. Beginning west of Yarnaby it rambled for a dozen or more miles through the countryside. For the lower 2/3 of its length, approximately, the creek followed the ancient Red River channel and cut through the old lakes named Grassy, Red, and Blue.

Several tributary creeks fed Brown's Creek, and these, in turn, could furnish good fishing. One of those creeks cut across our pasture and woods and behind our house only about fifty feet from our yard. Needless to say, it was a big part of my life as a boy. Two or three kinds of bream, creek cats, and goggle-eyes or green sunfish were the principle species. There were also occasional crappie and bass. Huge snapping turtles, big bull frogs, really big water snakes, fresh water clams or mussels, and giant red crawfish were also there.

This creek gave up plenty of suppers for my family, and as a bonus, along its banks there were patches of wild onions, and from decaying brush

5

piles farther from the banks, poke greens.

I learned much about the outdoors from this creek; fishing, hunting, gathering wild foods, observing and understanding the nature of wild critters, and learning to swim. This creek, is part of me to this day!

3 RED RIVER

River fishing also was good in these early days. The river, early in the summer, was usually turbid, even muddy, but if there were no heavy rains it generally cleared before the summer was over. Clear or muddy, Red River was a consistent producer of hump-back blue cats, sand bass, drum, and buffalo.

Favored baits were earthworms, yellow grasshoppers, shiners seined from the local creeks, and shrimp from the river itself. Big shad, when caught, were converted to cut-bait.

4 RIVER SHRIMP

When I was a boy my dad and his fishing cronies often went to the river. I enjoyed going along and one of my favorite things to do was helping catch bait with a minnow seine. In addition to shiners and shad, we frequently caught a bucket of river shrimp. These were the days before the completion and closing of Texoma Dam and the river ecology was much as it had been for eons of time. The river shrimp were abundant. Our easiest method of catching them was to place tumble-weeds in the edge of the river, then in about fifteen or twenty minutes lift the seine under the weeds and pull them out to the bank or simply raise the seine. A good haul might yield two or three-dozen shrimp from two to four inches long.

I've heard old-timers, veterans of fishing the river, tell about catching these river shrimp during flood times by using a light cane pole, hook and line, and baiting with a small piece of worm or bread. The most productive spots were along stands of flooded willows where current eddies caused foam to pile up. When shrimp were present a person could actually hear them snapping and clicking in the foam. Of course one had to be watchful for snakes and a very disconcerting by-catch might be a two or three foot long American eel.

These river shrimp, along with yellow grasshoppers from the fence row, were top baits for hump-back blue catfish up to six or eight pounds.

I haven't seen a big river shrimp for many years now, though I understand that the lower reaches of the Red and its final leg, the Atchafalaya, support a commercial fishery. I suspect that the closing of Texoma Dam marked the beginning of ecological changes which hastened their disappearance from the area.

My cousin, Carl, and I fished the river from the highway 78 bridge to the mouth of Island Bayou in the late 1950's through the early 1970's. In seining bait from overflow pools we frequently saw another shrimp species, transparent; hump-backed glass shrimp by the thousands- but never over one-half inch long.

5 EAGLE LAKE

On Easter Sunday, 1938, we loaded our tackle in Dad's Model A and headed for Eagle Lake. "We" included Dad, Mom, my baby sister, Doris, and my grandparents, Mamaw and Papaw. Dad's tackle included cane poles fastened to the side of the car, a couple of cans of red worms from the garden and his tackle box which was an old metal lunch box containing hooks, line, sinkers, cork floats, and a cord stringer.

The twelve mile trip from our home in Albany to the lake seemed to take forever. This was to be my first time to really seriously, fish! Papaw had filled a flat Prince Albert can with dirt and worms. This was my first bait can. He was my buddy that day. We rode to the lake in the rumble seat!

They set up a day camp in a grove of chinaberry trees on the north side of the lake where it began a long, graceful bend back to the east. Mom and Mamaw spread a quilt on the ground in the shade of the chinaberries, for Doris to play on. At noon we had a picnic lunch of fried chicken, beans cooked before we left home, fried potatoes, sliced onions and tomatoes from the garden, and corn bread. Home-churned butter and honey from Dad's hives added sweetness to our Easter dinner. Dad moved off to the east down the shoreline to fish around the stumps of trees from the land clearing that was happening in the river bottom at the time. Papaw and I rigged up a couple of poles and with worms from the tobacco can fished right there by camp.

It seems to me now, over a half century later, that I must have caught a hundred assorted bream and shiners: Probably not, but it was a bunch. My first fishing trip was a big success!

In its early history Eagle Lake was a typical ox-bow. Sometime, in the past in recent geological time, but ancient in people time, it had been a long, curving loop of the river. Red, in its endless meanderings, had finally taken the shortest route and simply cut off the loop and developed a shorter, straighter segment for its new channel. The distance around the loop, from where it leaves the river at the south end to the point at which it rejoins Red at the north end is close to three miles. In its prime its maximum width was probably a quarter of a mile. Over a period of hundreds of years, siltation has shortened and narrowed its bed. However, as recently as the 1970's, a person by being very observant could trace out the ancient boundaries. It's obvious that in ancient times it was a much larger body of water.

As recently as the 1940's it was still an impressive body of water. At the lower end of the lake (north) there were a number of isolated sloughs which marked the original path of the river and still became part of the lake during the flood season. At times these were good fishing holes. When the lake was young, before civilization took it down, it was the best around-a great fishing hole with a fishing camp, grocery store and post office at about its midpoint and fronting State Highway 78. The fishing camp had half dozen cabins and around two dozen rental boats. The lake was a good one, great fishing for several varieties of catfish, crappie, bream, buffalo, and drum. Enormous gars, including many alligator gar, as well as other species were present. Cover was abundant in the lake. The eastern shoreline was characterized by hundreds of willows in water up to four or five feet in depth during years of average rainfall.

Remnants from the sawmill venture, in the form of slab piles, were present around the northwest bend. Huge stumps, mostly from bois d'arc and cottonwood which were removed from the bottom land in clearing for agriculture, had been dumped in the shallow south end. All this made for ideal conditions for fishing for bass, crappie, and catfish.

6 LUNCH AT KARMA

Sometimes, when Dad and his buddies went to the river, they

would take me by the Karma store and leave me to go fish in Eagle Lake. I liked this because I'd catch lots of bream and also because he'd give me a quarter or fifty cents so I could buy lunch at the store. I'd usually have a cream soda or R C, a packet of crackers and a can of potted meat or vienna sausage. With this kind of lunch I was in gastronomic heaven. Mr. Charles Simmons, who ran the store, showed me a new kind of potted meat one day. It was Underwood's Deviled Ham. I was an instant fan of this new stuff! With a moon pie for dessert what more could any man want for a delicious meal!

 ## 7 BOAT BUILDERS

These four: Dad, Earl, the preacher, and Ed Haynie, decided to build their own boat. They thought it would be a smart thing to do since it would save the price of a boat rental at Eagle Lake. Most of the boats rented for fifty cents a day, except one--a steel boat! Woe to the fisherman who was late to the lake during the spring fishing season! The only boat left of the twenty or so that Charlie Simmons rented out was certain to be-this old steel tub. It was terrible to fish in. It was noisy, heavy and virtually impossible to paddle or row. It rented for only a quarter a day.

So the guys built a twelve foot flat-bottomed boat in their spare time. Carefully, they wet and heated the boards so as to get the right curvature. They carefully chinked the cracks and covered them with hot tar. Earl and the preacher, being carpenters, made a couple of paddles too.

Finally, the day arrived. The boat was finished--time to try it out. Earl's pick-up carried it to the lake. Charlie Simmons and some hangers-on at the Karma store gathered to watch the big launch. Earl and Ed Haynie were selected as the first passengers for this historic voyage. "It leaks a little" said Earl. "Not much though," said Haynie. "Maybe we'll put a little more tar in the cracks." Off they went, paddling north close to the shoreline, fortunately. Someone watching said, "It appears to be settling more into the water." "It is getting lower," someone else observed. "It's sinking!" Charlie Simmons said, and to the bottom it went. Just as it disappeared from view the two passengers disembarked, stepping into three feet of murky lake water. They slogged their way back to the landing, accompanied by hand claps and cheers from the on-lookers. So ended the great boat building project of Papa Earl and his friends. The boat now resides forever in the silt of the old lake.

8 THE GREAT RACE

Heavy spring rains had muddied Eagle Lake and the river. Earl, Dad, Preacher Amos, and Haynie headed for the river to fish for hump-back blue catfish. They'd seined crawdads for bait, and on the way, decided to go by the Karma store to aggravate Charlie Simmons. The ungravelled road from Highway 78 out to the store was a gumbo quagmire.

"Let's walk" said Papa Earl. "Let's cut across the field," said Preacher Amos, referring to the plowed but unplanted land between Highway 78 and the store. "Let's race," said Haynie. So off they went, lickety-split, for about twenty yards. By then they were bogged down in gumbo red clay to their knees. When they reached the store, carrying their shoes, the four of them looked like big old hogs, fresh from their favorite wallow.

9 THE HOUSEBOAT

A small houseboat came up the river that spring from Louisiana. They tied up to a sturdy willow near the run-out of the lake to the river. Haynie heard that the man and his wife were in dire straits. They had little food, no money, and she was ill. Haynie, Earl, my Dad, and the preacher took up a collection community wide, then they carried the money and some groceries to the couple. She was desperately ill. The four of them managed to carry her to Haynie's car and he drove her to a hospital in Durant. She died of pneumonia.

10 FLOOD SEASON

Most springs Eagle Lake swelled out of its bed, overflowing its banks into the surrounding fields. This was a result of flooding of the river which then overflowed into the lake, reclaiming it as another channel. When this flooding happened, big catfish, buffalo, and carp moved from the lake and river into the fields. Residents of the area would then go after the fish with hoes and pitchforks. My friend, Doug Bowen, and his brothers would have a high old time during such flood seasons. One of Doug's father's hounds was a great fish catcher. Once he got after a fish, he stayed with it until he caught it.

11 WADE FISHING

Earl and Dad had a favorite fishing area during springtime, near the south end of the lake. During low water, huge old bois d'arc stumps had been dumped there. These were a product of the clearing of land for farming around the lake. If the water level was just right, not too deep and with just the tops of the stumps showing, this became a fantastic spot to fish.

Their method of fishing was to use long cane poles and move slowly through the stump field. Their bait was shiners from our creek. As they waded; they eased a shiner gently around each bit of stump cover. The strings of fish they brought in were awesome. Once Dad had a six pound largemouth bass, several smaller ones and a huge stringer of big crappie. This catch was typical of Eagle Lake in its prime.

12 UNCLE CLARENCE'S BIG GAR

One summer, in the late 1930's, Uncle Clarence set a net for catfish in the willows along the far shore. He didn't catch any big cats but did catch an alligator gar which, on cotton scales, weighed 130 pounds. During the hard times of those Depression years, people were constantly on the look-out for chances to get together for good times and fun, and so it was decided that there would be a community fish fry with Clarence's gar being the guest of honor. The event would take place near the south end of the lake where low water had exposed a large area of clear lake bottom. Men brought their wagons and lanterns, their wives cooked pots of pinto beans and stacks of corn bread. Onions, peppers, and tomatoes from bottom-land gardens were cleaned and sliced. Mr. Qualls, the owner of the Karma store at that time, supplied ice for tea and white bread and canned peaches for dessert. Clarence, Papa Earl, and Lee butchered the gar. Surprisingly, the flesh was clean, white, and flaky. Slabs of it were rolled in corn meal and fried to a golden brown and were delicious! A great depression-era country party!

13 THE EAGLE LAKE SLOUGH

In the late 1930's and early 40' s, Earl and his family lived in a little white house east of Eagle Lake. His dad lived with the family for these few years. It has always been fascinating to me that Eurith and her sisters and brothers saw and talked to their grandfather who was born before the Civil War.

Earl often said that this place near Eagle Lake was a good place in which to live. There was a good garden spot and a small orchard with a variety of fruit trees. Just south of the house there was a good-sized slough of a couple of acres. It never went dry and during the years of flood, it simply became a part of the lake which carried flood waters east to the main river channel. Eagle Lake at these times was a chute reclaimed by Red which spilled over at the south end into the lake.

A result of this flood season was the annual restocking of the slough with a variety of fish that were very good to eat. Earl often described to me the big black perch he cane-poled from it. He also said that he fed the family during these late Depression years on catfish he caught on a trot-line that he kept strung across the shallower east end of the slough. These catfish included channels and some enormous mud cats. He said the mud cats often attained weights of two or three pounds and were just as welcome to the family table as were the more highly regarded channel catfish.

14 DEAD MAN'S LAKE

This lake was just another bend in the river until sometime in the 1930's. There was a settlement of sorts along the river and several families, including a couple of my uncles, farmed the rich land. It was a losing proposition though (even heart-breaking) because the river, during flood time, would claim many acres of bottom land. At times entire fields of corn or cotton would cave away as the current attacked the banks.

Finally, the farmers gave up and moved away to less destructive areas. Sometime during the late 30's the river made a meander which left a big loop as a cut-off of several hundred acres. I've no real knowledge of exactly when this happened but suspect it was around 1937 when there was a huge flood of the Mississippi and its southern tributaries.

Dead Man's Lake got its name as a result of a tragedy occurring in the construction of Texoma Dam in the 1940's. A worker on the powerhouse that was being constructed fell off a scaffold into the raging current during the spring flood time. His body was recovered many days later in a bend of the river cut-off many miles downstream. As a result, the cut-off became popularly known as Dead Man's Lake and appears as such in the quadrangle maps of the U. S. Department of the Interior. For years now, it has been called simply, Dead Lake.

In February, 1958, my Dad and I, Eurith's dad, Earl and her Uncle Henry made a fishing trip to Dead Lake. The cut-off was almost dry with only a channel of water flowing through the center. We fished the lower end around some dead-falls, without much success, just a few small bass and several bream of various kinds. The land on the north shore had been recleared of timber that had grown up during the 40's and much of the downed forest had been pushed by dozers into the lake bed.

In the summer of 1958, Eurith's family camped, on a cat-fishing trip to the river, in an area along the river just north of the lake. Another meander of the big stream had brought the main channel back to the Oklahoma side and the mouth of the lake opened up right into the river. It looked fishy but we didn't have much luck for catfish or bass.

Our camp was in a patch of giant ragweed just yards from the river, good territory for rattlers! We didn't sleep a lot that first night. The mouth of a stream, Island Bayou, was only about a half mile from that of Dead Lake. The entire area was heavily wooded with only a small amount of agricultural clearing. This region was rich in wildlife and game. Deer were still frequently seen during this time and there were rumors of occasional sightings of cougar and bear.

Eurith and I, during this summer of 1958, fished almost everywhere around the river, her pregnancy not withstanding! We put out limb lines in the Bayou, downstream from the Albany Bridge. There were some things that were very strange about the stream. The water was surprisingly clear, almost crystal clear, and seemingly as cold as ice water. I caught a number of catfish and a huge snapping turtle. The cats I caught included a few channels and some unusual looking bull heads--much different from those I'd been accustomed to from the creeks around home. Their heads were flattened, and they were brownish in color without rounded tail fins. They were obviously not the common flathead or yellow cat which reaches an enormous size.

A few years later, <u>Florida Wildlife</u> which I subscribed to had an article about the smaller members of the catfish family and one of the species featured was the flat bullhead or snail cat which according to the picture and description seemed to be identical to my Island Bayou cats. It seems improbable that these fish would be found, naturally, several hundred miles west of their normal range. But years later in Dead Lake, I frequently observed a snake species of the genus Natrix which is another animal of southeastern habitat. The Red River ecology, in those days, at least, was unique!

I didn't return to Dead Lake until July, 1968 when Carl, Frank, another cousin, and I decided to check it out. Frank had heard that one of the Potts boys had caught over forty bass in a couple of hours. So Carl brought his boat and trailer and somehow we managed to launch off the north shore.

I couldn't believe how much the lake had changed since the 1958 trips. Instead of a bare lake bed which filled only during high water release times from Texoma Dam, there was obviously a permanent body of water, a "wetland." It was choked with cattails and coontail moss, but was alive with red wing blackbirds, turtles, bullfrogs, and an enormous number and variety of water snakes, including some huge cottonmouths. We saw several of these that appeared as large as a man's leg-- scary!!

Our fishing trip was a bust, we only caught three or four bass, but the experience was interesting and fun, to say the least. The lake was very shallow and Carl's V bottom boat was not the best boat for fishing it. We paddled and pushed, and wallowed through the cattails and moss until we'd had enough.

Dad and I fished the lake in January of 1970. Some big changes had occurred. For some reason, the cattail marsh was now a beautiful open-water lake. The cattails had disappeared. I'm not certain about the reason, but have since learned that this plant can become afflicted with diseases that literally destroy entire populations. In all the later trips I made to the lake through 1980, unbelievably, I never saw another cattail. There was plenty of coontail moss and during the summer of that year the lake became pretty well choked with it. However, there was still a lot of open, fishable water and several channels which for some reason, were clear of the moss. Later, I found carp and buffalo clearing such openings.

Carl and I fished Dead Lake several times during that summer of 1970. We did a lot of exploring and finally began to understand the nature of the lake and its geography. My knowledge of the Dead Lake area as it was in the 70's is a result of boat explorations on fishing trips, and of "walk-arounds" during hunting seasons in the fall and winter. The water level was maintained by two things; the dike which was man-made with bulldozers, and the beaver dam across the main channel at the east end of· the lake.

The dike had been constructed in order to enable a land owner to claim some of the beach area as his own, the intention being to farm or pasture it. As far as I know it was only pastured, and very lightly at that. The large beaver dam across the main channel was about four feet high. It permitted a constant though variable flow of water northeasterly through a channel to the river. I've walked this out during the cold weather hunting season and discovered some interesting facts about it. Along its course the channel spreads out, in low areas, into small ponds. The channel and ponds are heavily populated with muskrats and, at times, with ducks and geese. I've seen them covered with water fowl. I think it's possible for there to be a small population of alligators in this area, considering its wildness, remoteness, and the presence of other species usually considered to be indigenous to the southeastern United State.

. The river bed itself is a wilderness area and is a terrific wildlife habitat. Grown up in tamarisk or salt cedar, willow, red cedar, bag pod, coffee bean, sumac, partridge pea, lespedeza and countless other species of plants, it is rich in food and cover. Ideal habitat for waterfowl along its ponds and waterways, it also has traditionally supported a heavy quail population.

Of course, evidence of the origins of this area is obvious. A person so inclined can "walk out" many 'of the old chutes and channels which may presently be a mile or more from the river itself. On one of our hunting forays I found a relic remnant of a very large, old wooden row-boat half filled with sand and probably at least a half mile from the river!

In June 1978 Carl and I made a bass fishing trip to the lake. This time we loaded my twelve foot jon boat into the pick-up, packed a lunch, ice chest and a good assortment of small spinner baits and top water lures. Our goal was the "finger lakes" south of the main body of water. I'd checked this out during my "walk arounds" of the previous fall hunting season. It sure looked bassy to me:

Getting to the "finger lakes" was not so easy. We drove as far as possible to the east end of the lake, launched the boat and began paddling through the narrow channel toward the beaver dam. There were deadfalls across the channel and only God knows how many snakes along the bank and swimming behind, alongside of, and in front of the boat. Carl had brought a .22 pistol as snake protection, but we quickly discarded that idea. Instead, we decided to "live with" them and just watch carefully. For our amusement we started counting them but quickly gave up on this--too many! We finally settled for counting only the snakes that swam across in front of the boat, and we gave up on that when the count reached forty, somewhat disconcerting in a jon boat with a twelve inch transom!

In the boat, besides the two of us, we had two rods each, a styrofoam ice chest, a paddle each (not oars) and a small tackle box apiece. We developed a system for getting over the landfalls. Carl, in the bow, stepped on the log, after judiciously inspecting it for you know what, then pulled the boat up on the log as far as possible. Then I stepped out onto the log, we pushed and pulled the boat on over, he got in, and then so did I.

On a later trip we decided to bring a handsaw to cut smaller deadfalls. After cutting through a couple, we decided it was too time consuming and that our original method was best.

During this first finger-lake trip as we paddled down the south channel we discovered another, smaller beaver dam. It was pretty solid, a structure of limbs and mud easily supporting a man's weight. The beavers had thoughtfully left a notch in the center through which the boat could easily be pulled. However on this first trip, it was guarded by one of the biggest, fattest cottonmouths I've ever seen. He was apparently quite happy to see us as he gave us a big grin, exposing the pure white mouth lining typical of his kind. "I'm not going anywhere," he seemed to say, "are you?"

After talking it over, we decided to respect his property rights, paddled to the east end of the dam, carefully stepped out and carried the boat around. Hours later, as we reversed our pathway, old no-shoulders couldn't be seen. You can bet we moved very carefully!

The eastern-most of the finger lakes seemed most inviting. There seemed to be five or six feet of depth along much of its length which probably was around a hundred yards. Button bushes and willows pushed in from the sides and there were numerous tree tops in the water. Everywhere there was evidence of fish: bream, small bass, shiners, shad, and dragonflies. We tried a variety of baits like tiny torpedoes, devil's horse and spinner baits. Nothing worked. Discouraging. About 11 o'clock the dragonflies began their mating swarm, depositing their eggs in the coontail moss at or near the surface. Suddenly. the bass went crazy! Even two or three pounders would leap after the insects. We caught them on top waters until we were exhausted.

Finally, after about an hour and a half of this the action tapered off. We switched to spinner baits. I chose a small, black-skirted H & H, skirt reversed, of course we could see the bass charge out of the moss as the spinner slowly whisked by. This was bass fishing at its most elemental, basic level, terrific! One enormous bass savagely attacked my H & H. I had the bass fishing fight of my life, trying to keep him out of the moss and brush piles. Later, he weighed five and half pounds and "was twenty-one inches long, not a big fish when compared to today's Florida strain, man-made lake, mass produced specimens, but a terrific, wild, native bass trophy.

Carl and I fished Dead Lake many times after this and developed a reliable, productive pattern. We found that it wasn't always necessary to be there at daylight. The dragonfly "hatch" was the determining factor, to a large degree. So we learned to time our arrival to coincide with its beginning. We discovered another pattern. As the summer went on and the moss became thicker, the fishing got tougher, as expected. But, no matter how much moss, there were always some small openings of moss-free water. We called these "peep holes" because we found that a small top water lure, carefully cast into them, would as often as not elicit a savage strike and these solitary fish were generally much larger than the dragon fly chasers. Rarely did we make a trip without catching at least one four to five pound fish each by using this method.

The top-water baits that seemed best, to us at least, were small Tiny Torpedoes, in yellow or frog-patterns. Small sized 1/4 ounce Dalton Specials and 1/8 ounce Hula Poppers were just as good. My favorite was the Devil's toothpick, smallest of the Horse tribe, without a tail spinner but weighted so as to sit upright in the water. A slight twitch would cause the tooth-pick to move vertically, dip, but not horizontally--perfect for fishing the peep holes.

We developed a set of rods and reels that seemed ideal for this type of fishing. I started with an Ambassadeur 5000, 15 pound line, and a 5

17

foot 8 inch Shakespeare rod. A good outfit, but I put together a better one. The reel, a 1928 direct drive, with 12 lb. braided nylon, 15 lb. leader, 5 1/2 foot Heddon Pro-lite rod. The advantage being that often a bass would instantly hit the plug once it hit the water. The free spool Ambassadeur just wasn't fast enough to hit every strike, the direct drive Shakespeare was! The braided nylon was easier to manage, without a backlash under these conditions and the little Heddon rod was light and fast. The 5000 and wonder rod became my back-up. Carl used similar tackle but tended to favor a spin-caster for his light Hula Poppers--deadly!

In those days, the 1970's, Dead Lake had approximately thirty or forty acres of open water in the main body. The numerous side channels and finger lakes increased the acreage somewhat. The upper end curved back toward the river, had water for quite a distance and then gradually faded out into a swag or low area and eventually opened up at the bank of the river. This swag was dry land most of the time, or at least simply moist land. In the hunting season its edges were a good quail hunting area. Strangely enough, during the cooler months, it was a gathering area for woodcock. I'm not certain if those timber doodles were there for the winter or just making a rest stop on their way to the Louisiana swamps. When quail hunting, Dad and I made occasional forays into the swag and usually added one or two to our game bags.

In flood time, if the river overflowed its banks, it came roaring through the swag making the lake simply another river bed. After such a season I've seen coontail moss strands attached to willow limbs fifteen to twenty feet above the normal water level. Probably these floods were good since they flushed out a lot of the moss and perhaps freshened the lake by removing some of the silt that accumulated from the small area of cultivated land along the north shore.

On one trip I made after such a flood time in 1977 I found, numerous small, dead, paddlefish lying on top of the moss. They were uniform in size, ten inches long, and were just freshly dead. I reasoned that probably a school of immature fish had been trapped when the flood waters receded and were unable to cope with the sulfide rich lake waters as they warmed.

Even though the coontail constantly threatened to choke the lake, it was also its savior. During the heat of summer when surface temperatures were very high a hand thrust through the moss would encounter water as seemingly cold as ice. It wasn't, of course, but must have been many degrees cooler than the surface.

The lake was loaded with a variety of fish besides bass. There were several varieties of bream, both white and black crappie, shad, shiners, and an assortment of rough fish, carp, buffalo, and thousands of spotted gar averaging a pound or two in weight. These gar were beautiful little fish and were perfectly willing to strike a small top water plug. On one trip my dad and I had fished our usual bass spots with good success, around a dozen or two bass each, and were paddling back to the boat launch when we saw a lot of surface activity at the mud shoal produced by drainage siltation from the soybean field along the north shore. We paddled as fast as we could to the disturbance and found that a mix of bass and gar had hemmed a bunch of forage fish, shad and shiners, against the shoal and were ripping them to shreds. Some of the gar were big ones, looking to be around eight to ten pounds or perhaps larger. We had a ball with the top waters catching both bass and gar up to around four pounds.

An average trip to Dead Lake would produce around a dozen bass each for the two of us. We often would take a fly-rod and tried small poppers. They worked fine for bream, small bass, and an occasional crappie.

On a trip that Carl and I made in June of 1976, we caught forty bass up to four pounds and lost four big ones that burrowed into the moss. That was our top trip for numbers. We released practically all the fish we caught on these trips, rarely keeping three or four for a meal.

I've never seen bass in such good condition as these wild ones. They had small heads, fat football-shaped bodies and their fight or the light tackle we used could be rest described as "exuberant."

As I've mentioned before, there was a small acreage of cultivated land along the north shore and quite a bit of open pasture land on the west side as the lake curved back to the south. The south and east sides were a wilderness, huge willows along the shore, then giant oaks, cottonwood, and along the sandy areas of the old river beach, some of the largest, most beautiful cedars I've ever seen. There were several beaver "slides" along the south shore and an abundance of musk-rat dens.

As the years passed, conditions changed considerably both with respect to access and to the ecology. In 1981, Dad and I made our last trip to the lake. We caught a few bass and the lake still looked pretty good but I think that we both sensed that this was the last trip.

Dead Lake is still there, though access to it is not. I think of it often and have many special memories of the fish and of the good times with Dad and Carl.

 ## 15 SUMMER STORM

On a July day in 1961 my cousin Carl and I pulled up to the slough bank, waded the lower end of the slough and headed down the beach to where Red River made a sharp turn to the right toward the Texas bank. The swift current had gouged a deep hole into the bottom against the bank on our side. A sizable bois d'arc had washed into the hole and had partially sanded under. With this cover and deep water, a potential hot-spot had been created

My dad and I had fished the spot a couple of days earlier using river shiners I had jugged, and had caught a couple of two pound channel cats, and a dozen sand bass. Dad had also landed a beautiful flathead of five pounds. Carl and I hoped our trip this day would be equally productive.

Carl tried the old reliable Shyster spinner while I set up the jugs for shiners. After about half an hour I'd caught a couple of dozen shiners and Carl had landed three or four nice sandies by casting the spinner into the swift current and retrieving slowly.

We baited up with the live shiners and began working the hole around the bois d'arc brush pile. Action was slow and after an hour of fishing we'd caught a couple of small sandies each. The day, which had started clear and hot, became sultry and hotter. A dark summer thunderstorm cloud began forming southwest of us, and we agreed that we'd better watch the storm, but kept fishing. As often happens during such weather changes, the fishing really turned on. In the next half-hour we caught a dozen or more nice sandies and a couple of keeper channel cats. We sort of lost interest in the thunderstorm.

Suddenly, the storm gained our attention, fast! A dark, dark cloud with jagged, brilliant lightning flashes was headed right towards us and seemed to be less than a half mile away! Without a word, we reeled in our tackle, collected our gear, and fish-loaded stringers, and headed for the car a half mile across the beach.

We walked fast, burdened by our tackle and fish and seemed to be gaining ground on the storm. Suddenly, as if it were a black monster with a mind of its own, this hot little cloud began throwing thunderbolts of lightning in defiance of our escape efforts, and then it took a short cut. While we were at an angle southeast of the car and safety, the storm took a direct path in an apparent effort to head us off. Desperately, we tried to out-run it but with the load of tackle, the fish, and the loose sand, found that to be an impossibility. "Hit the dirt", Carl said as a thunderbolt sizzled into the earth a hundred yards south of us and ice cold rain began pelting us. "Let's make a lightning rod", I said and propped our casting rods on salt cedars a few yards from us. Knowing that taller objects are most likely to draw lightning strikes, we squinched down into the sand as much as possible. Things were really getting hot now! Lightning bolts were crackling and cold rain drops were peppering us. We dug into the loose beach sand, burying ourselves, even putting our caps over our faces and covering our heads! A deluge soaked the sand, and us! Lightning crackled and popped. Our bodies tingled with each strike.

Suddenly, the summer storm moved on after having turned its fury on us. We dug ourselves out of the sand. Two more wretched looking, sand covered, soaking wet fools of fishermen could not have been found! Our tackle was full of sand; our fish were covered in it. My watch told me that the whole thing hadn't lasted more than ten minutes. That was enough!

We slowly made our way toward the slough and the car. We stopped in the slough and tried to wash off the sand encrusting ourselves, finally gave up, clambered up the bank to the car and headed home. Two drowned, sandy rats, laughing about our day's fishing!

16 FATTY FITZPATRICK AND THE FISHING FENCE

In those days, the 1940s, Fatty's family lived in an old log house on the bank of Eagle Lake, an oxbow of Red River, separating Oklahoma and Texas. The log house was once the "big house" of the Millar plantation in the Red River bottom.

Fatty, Jerald, and I loved to fish in Eagle Lake. Our favorite spot was an old board fence that was built when the lake was at a low level. When the lake was full the pig-lot with the fence around it was about three or four feet deep in water and the pigs had to be kept in the barn next to the lot.

The three of us loved to climb out on the fence with our fishing poles and sit on the posts and fish. Our bait was worms: earthworms, and white grub worms. Sometimes we used grasshoppers and crickets. We'd catch a variety of fish, mostly red-bellied bream and mud catfish. Sometimes we caught drum and crappie.

One day Jerald and I rode our bikes the two and a half miles to Fatty's house on the lake. We took our fishing poles, stringers to put the fish on, and a tow sack to carry the fish home.

Fatty and his four sisters were picking up potatoes in the family garden. Fatty's mother told us, "If you'll help finish picking up potatoes he can go fishing with you."

We spread the potatoes on the floor of a building called a smokehouse. They would dry out and keep for months without rotting. They had already gathered their onion crop and the onions were tied in bunches of a dozen or so to the rafters in the smoke house. Some of the onions were huge, weighing a pound or more. Things really grew in that river bottom soil.

About the middle of the morning we finished the potato job and started to go to our fence. "Elwood", Fatty's mother said. "If you fall in and get your clothes wet again I'll take a switch to your bottom". She always called him Elwood. We didn't understand why. We always called him Fatty and thought that was his name.

We climbed out on the fence, carefully, because we had to watch for snakes, If any were on the fence we'd shoo them away with a few prods from our fishing poles. We seated ourselves on our favorite posts and commenced fishing. We were pretty quiet, for nine year old guys, and were rapidly adding perch and little catfish to our stringers.

THEN IT HAPPENED! A big, old, fat, yellow-bellied water snake swam down the fence right under our feet toward a big willow tree to our left. Fatty happened to look down just as the snake came by. "Yee-ow", he squealed and KERSPLASH he went as he fell backward off the fence into the lake. It's hard to say if Fatty or the snake was scared the most.

Jerald and I laughed so hard that we almost fell off, too. "I'm in trouble now," Fatty said, almost in tears. "Mama will switch me real good".

We had a conference about the situation. "Fatty," Jerald said, "Why don't you spread your clothes on the fence to dry? Your mother won't know you fell in." Fatty thought about this for a little while. He said,

"If I do that I'll be nekkid as a jay bird and you guys will laugh at me all day". He probably was right, but we told him we'd hang our clothes on the fence, too, if it would make him feel better. "OK" he said. And we did. So there we were, three naked nine year olds, fishing away while Fatty's clothes dried in the warm sun.

After a while our stringers were full and we decided to go ride our bikes in the dusty road that ran along the lake shore.

We began to put on our clothes to go do our thing with the bikes. Suddenly, there was a soft splash, a squall of frustration, and a bigger KERSPLASH as Fatty fell off the fence again. Old yellow belly had decided to go back to his first willow tree, and his first trip being so much fun, he took the same route right along the fence and right under our feet again. Fatty had been busy with his clothes, and when he saw the snake come by again he was so startled that he dropped them. In grabbing for them he'd lost his balance and fallen in.

So there we were, Jerald and I laughing our heads off and Fatty in tears! I was laughing so hard at Fatty's predicament that I lost my balance and KERSPLASH again. I was wet, my clothes were wet, and Jerald was laughing at both of us. Fatty and I looked at each other, nodded our heads at Jerald, and without a word, up-ended him into the lake. All the laughing, whooping, hollering, and splashing probably made old yellow belly wish he'd taken another route to his willow tree.

After a while we decided to go on and ride our bikes. We fixed our full stringers of perch and catfish to the fence. Later we'd collect them, put them in the wet tow sacks and carry them home for supper. We had a lot of fun on our bikes: wheelies, spin-outs, and quite a few fall-downs. The combination of wet clothes and red road dust had us looking like mud turtles as we collected our fish and tackle and headed home. We were really tired after all the excitement of the day.

"What in the world has happened to you?" Mama said when I came home. In my best nine year old way I told her of the happenings of the day. "Go to the creek, jump in and wash your clothes and yourself" she said, somewhat unclearly, because she was having a little trouble talking for some reason. Her mouth was twitching. Her shoulders were shaking a little, and once she even burst into laughter.

For supper we had fresh fried fish, corn bread, butter beans, okra, and sliced tomatoes from the garden. She made our favorite dessert:

pineapple upside down cake. It was really a good supper.

I went to bed earlier than usual that night. Just as I was drifting off to sleep I heard Mama and Daddy talking. For some reason their talk was mixed with a lot of giggles and laughing. I wondered what they were talking about but was too tired to think about it much.

17 CATFISHING

During one of our trips to the river in 1970, Dad and I came across one of his old friends, Brad Martin. We were walking down the river-side trail to a spot near the Dead Lake swag that we liked to fish when we spotted Brad at the water's edge near a submerged bois d'arc brush pile. He was holding a casting rod of seven and a half or eight feet long and the rod was sharply bent as Brad attempted to lift a fish from the entangling brush.

We watched silently as he finally worked a lunker catfish to the shore and Dad secured him using Brad's landing net. The fish was a solid specimen of around ten pounds.

"That's a good one," Dad said, "How've you been doing, Brad?" "Good to see you'all," Brad replied, "This is my biggest today. Yesterday I caught four fish including an eighteen pound blue from this same brush pile."

He lifted his stringer to show his day's catch. In addition to the ten pounder he'd just landed, he had three smaller cats of about one and half to two and half pounds. All were fat humpbacked blues. Brad showed us his method of fishing. The casting rod had a reel that was a light Penn #9 and was loaded with 25 pound monofilament. He used no leader and his sinker, a one ounce egg style, slid down to the eye of a 2/0 heavy duty Eagle Claw bait holder hook. A piece of sponge covered the bend of the hook, but the point was exposed.

Brad said, "What are you'll using for bait?" Dad told him that we had crawfish we'd seined and a cage of yellow grasshoppers I'd caught the night before.

"Those are good baits" Brad replied, "but I've had better luck lately with this stink bait." He used a stick to press the water from the sponge on the hook, then pushed the affair into a quart jar of vile looking stuff, that to put it mildly, had a distinctive aroma. "I've about quit using anything for cats except this," he added. "Where do you buy it?" Dad asked.

"Well, Mr Knight has some in his bait shop," Brad replied, referring to the shop in Durant where we usually stopped to buy minnows when on our way to Texoma to fish for crappie. "But it's a little different from this. It's good bait but I've found that this is better. A fellow from Cobb gave me the recipe for this." Brad went on to give Dad the list of ingredients and finished by saying that he let the mixture cure for three days or longer before using it.

The next day, Dad drove to Durant and came back with calf brains, limburger cheese, a package of strong cheddar cheese, and a pound of beef melt. Beef melt is the layer of fat which is trimmed off the kidneys at the butcher shop. I'd told Dad that if he got the ingredients I'd mix it. So we got out the old sausage grinder from the smokehouse and I proceeded to grind. We had enough of the mess to half-fill a gallon glass jar. We agreed that the lid should be loose so that no explosion of the bait would occur. I carried it out to the old chicken house, now empty of chickens, and placed it on a shelf to cure out.

Dad had used stink bait for catfish for many years but had used it entirely during the winter months. His method had been to buy a jar of dead minnows from the bait dealer, Mr. Knight. These were simply the dead soldiers that Mr. Knight had skimmed from his minnow vats, placed in jars, and kept in the refrigerator in the bait shop. When Dad would return home with a couple of the jars, he'd bury them in the back yard. After four or five days they'd be ready to use. He liked to use a long cane pole for this style of fishing. At the end of his line he tied a treble hook holding a piece of sponge. A heavy sinker of about an ounce was fastened to his line just above the sponge. The bait was stirred thoroughly. Then the sponge covered treble was pushed with a stick into the bait. Dad's favorite fishing spots included areas with plenty of brush, like Brad's. He'd walk the river bank dipping his baited hook into likely looking spots. With the long pole he could thoroughly work out the brush piles. For this kind of fishing he preferred Blue River, a tributary of the Red. Blue River was much narrower and usually had plenty of brush piles and drifts. During years of high water from floods it became loaded with cats from the Red.

We used Brad's version of the stink bait off and on for the rest of the summer in Red River, and did well with it. Seldom did we fail to catch at least a few catfish, but no real lunkers. In time we forgot about the stink bait

25

as we concentrated on sandies and blacks in Texoma, hitting them heavily with shad-like lures such as Hot Spots and Gay Blades on weekends during the fall.

During Christmas break of 1970, Dad and his new wife and a couple of her sons went to the coast. Eurith, our kids, and I stayed behind to watch after the place and keep the livestock fed. My plans were to hunt quail and fish in some ponds or below the Texoma Dam.

One bright, crisp day I filled a pint jar with stink bait from Brad's recipe, grabbed my tackle and drove down to the beer joints on the river. Leaving my pick-up in the deserted parking lot, I walked the half mile or so to the main river channel. My goal was a likely looking brush pile I'd seen while quail hunting a couple of days earlier.

After reaching the brush pile I baited up with a generous wad of the jar's contents. I gently lobbed a cast under the visible brush. The water was clean and cold and I started to set down on a nearby log to do some relaxed fishing. No relaxation here though! After only a few minutes of soaking my bait I had a wicked, strong strike. I set my hook and the battle was on! The catfish tried desperately to entangle me in the brush but I luckily was able to avoid that. After a give and take battle that seemed like fifteen minutes but was actually only a couple, I succeeded in landing my prize, a fat, beautiful cat that later at home, pulled the De-Liar to the seven pound mark!

Before calling it a day, I caught two more channels, a four pounder and a six pounder. These three cats, in a wet tow sack were about all I wanted to tote to the pickup, over a half mile away.

The stink baits I use today in my occasional cat fishing forays are very similar to the one from Brad Martin's recipe. Most of the modern baits have binding material added such as Cattail pollen and fibers. These seem best although some makers use cotton fibers or even man-made ones. Such a bait is "punch" instead of the dipping style we used. Good quality stink bait is one of the surest ways of catching a mess of catfish.

18 THE BEER JOINT LAKE

The approach to the Highway 78 bridge linking Oklahoma and Texas was destroyed in the 1930's during a couple of years of heavy flooding. The main river channel was against the Oklahoma bank. The channel now under the bridge was only secondary at that time. Access to Bonham, Texas or Durant, Oklahoma was, for years, confined to the Carpenter's Bluff bridge or the bridge north of Denison, Texas.

The vast area west of the Highway 78 bridge was superb wildlife habitat. No serious attempt to farm or pasture the beach area was undertaken, for it overflowed virtually every year. Back from the beach area the bottomland forest had been cleared, during the 20's and 30's primarily, though isolated patches persisted until the early 50's. The resulting agricultural land was some of the richest in the country with red topsoil many yards thick. Corn and cotton crops could be prodigious in good years.

Wildlife, during this time, was abundant and much water fowl hunting occurred in the fall and winter months. Eagle Lake was one of the best fishing holes around and the Red River was a tremendous fishing stream, as were its tributaries. The frequent floods that occurred were a disaster and at the same time a blessing for the farmer and the wildlife. During high water periods Red ate away at its banks, destroying entire fields of cultivated crops. Non-flood years in which there was adequate rainfall were times of plenty. But such years were rare, and many farm families near the river had their hearts broken year after year until they finally left the area. As a result of this and other economic factors most of the farmable river land from Highway 78 east to the mouth of Blue River was owned by a relatively small number of individuals.

The effects of the flooding were good for the topsoil and for fish and wildlife. The floodwaters deposited layers of silt over existing farm land. This was like a tremendous shot of fertilizer to the land and accounted for the existence of such topsoil in the first place. Flooding also increases the feeding and spawning areas for the fishes of the river. Many old sloughs, oxbows, and other types of depressions fill with water, and at least temporarily, became occupied by a wide assortment of catfish, bass, bream, buffalo, carp, and their prey, the forage fishes such as shad, river shiners, suckers, etc. The flood helps permanent residents of the river lakes such Eagle Lake and Dead Lake by flushing out excess vegetation and removing excessive amounts of silt.

In 1947 a new permanent earthen dike approach to the Highway 78 bridge was completed. This was the death blow for Eagle Lake as a viable fishery. One of the landowners brought in bull-dozers. A ditch was dug, and

27

the lake was drained. Supposedly, the drainage was to allow the lake bed to be farmed. This never happened, and, to this year, 2012, Eagle Lake remains a wetland, too dry for fish, too wet to plow. It still is used extensively by waterfowl, possibly to their detriment because the lake waters are almost certainly contaminated by agricultural chemicals. As far as I know no studies have ever been conducted upon the ecology of the area to check this out.

The completion of the Highway 78 bridge work was accompanied by opening up the channel under the bridge proper as the main channel and the partial closure of the Oklahoma channel. The new bridge approach divided the Oklahoma channel into two back-water lakes. The west one was smaller and since the torrential current of the river's flood was denied to it, it began to silt in rather quickly. For several years it was used by fishermen fishing from the bank or from small boats. There was some cover for fish. Steel Quads about eight ten feet tall had been placed along the beach area of the old channel back in the 1930's. These were supposed to function as a collective jetty, and there were hundreds of them. The idea was to use them to reduce bank erosion. It was a bad idea. It didn't work and the quads were rolled about to random positions by floodwaters. After the old channel became a back water lake, the quads became fishing hot spots. In addition, many willows grew along the shoreline and were felled by beavers, also hot spots.

In the 1950's I fished several times in this west lake, usually with my father-in-law in his flat-bottom boat. I've caught mostly small bass and decent crappie. The east lake, on the other side of the Highway 78 approach was a much better fishing hole.

By 1948, the Eagle Lake drainage had been broadened to approximately fifty yards with a creek-like channel in the middle. This channel seemed constantly to have a stream of clear water running through it. Willows had sprung up all around the area and there were some deep holes, up to six or seven feet near the mouth of the run-out. These became good fishing spots for crappie.

This east lake, which became known as the beer joint lake, received water from Red River at its east end as well as run-off from the surrounding farm land through Eagle Lake. No more did the torrential flood-time river come blasting through this channel. It was effectively blocked off by the man-made barriers resulting from construction of the highway dike to the 18 bridge.

When the Red was high, this lake was also. At times it had as much as fifteen or twenty feet of water depth, was close to a mile in length and probably a hundred fifty yards-wide. Over the years its water level stabilized at about seven feet in the deepest part and three to five feet over the rest of it. Beavers constructed a massive dam at the east or river end and like most beaver dams there was generally a constant flow of water through it. This, plus spillover from the Red at high water level insured that fish could constantly trade back and forth between the lake and river. This lake quickly acquired a solid reputation locally as a good producer of crappie- and catfish.

Our local Boy Scout troop, in 1949 or 1950, undertook a community improvement project. The Troop built a large raft of willow and cottonwood logs and heavy sawmill boards. The older, more mature members of the troop took the project in hand and with the help of the younger members who were novices at such work, did a fantastic job of construction. When finished the raft was approximately twenty by thirty feet and had support floatation consisting of sealed steel barrels firmly tied in place. It was solidly anchored with two steel cables tied to massive live willow trees several yards back from the water's edge. The lake depth around the raft averaged about six to eight feet. This raft was used extensively as a fixed fishing barge by local fishermen. With the addition of cedar tree brush piles, it became a crappie hot-spot, particularly at night.

As expected the lake began to silt in because of run-off from surrounding farm land but the fishing remained good for crappie for several years. The enormous flood of 1957 filled the beer joint lake and backed up into Eagle Lake. The raft finally floated free from its mooring during the flood, and when the waters receded it was perched atop a big drift at the lower end of the lake, and was no longer usable by fishermen. The quality of construction was evident though, it remained intact with its rusting cables until the early 1970's when it finally fell apart. The raft lasted longer than the Boy Scout Troop of Yuba which constructed it.

In 1954, I fished many times in the beer joint lake, mostly for bream and crappie. One day, I took a couple of cane poles, a bucket of shiners, and a can of red worms to the lake in my Dad's old pick-up. The two sons of the land-owner had welded two car hoods together and made a boat, of sorts. The boat was left on the lake shore for public use. This day I carefully flipped the boat over, so as not to surprise any cotton mouths resting under it, and slid it into the lake. I paddled to a spot where a couple of car bodies had been

29

dumped where there were some big shoreline willows. Lodged in the roots of the willows and projecting into the lake at a right angle to the far shore was a huge old cedar log, the root end out into the lake. I tied up to a snag near the end of the log, baited up and began fishing.

Crappie were swarming in the lake at this time. They weren't large, the biggest being about ten inches, occasionally a twelve inch lunker, but most were around eight or nine inches. Certainly, they were good pan-sized fish. By noon I'd used up all my worms, had been reduced to cutting my shiners into small pieces for cut bait and used them up, too. Then I began using cut-up crappie. I'm sure jigs would have been perfect this day but I'd neglected bringing any. No matter, by 3 o'clock I'd caught over a hundred crappie and had culled to forty keepers plus a dozen big bream and a single channel cat of a couple of pounds; a terrific day of pan-fishing, but not unusual for this lake.

In the flood of '57, this beer joint lake was filled to overflowing and backed water into Eagle Lake to a depth of several feet. Catfish, bass, carp, buffalo, and gar were now free to roam, feed, and spawn throughout several hundred acres of vegetation filled with new water. A sand pit from which fill for the Highway 78 dike had been taken ten years earlier filled with the overflow and with fish! A rumor circulated around Yuba that a fellow from Bonham had caught a nine pound largemouth bass from the pit, which was just south of the lake.

Fish were hard to locate though. I made several trips to the beer joint lake, fishing the west end of it since the Eagle Lake run-out was filled with approximately fifteen feet of standing water, making the eastern part of the lake inaccessible. On one occasion, fishing around the old dumped car bodies, my Dad and I caught a couple of dozen nice crappie of one to one and a half pounds-- big crappie, for this water. But like the other fish, the crappie seemed to be moving around and were difficult to find. Subsequent trips yielded only four or five small fish plus one or two larger ones. Finally, the crappie moved out or simply quit biting.

One day, using red worms around the abandoned cars, I was unable to get so much as a nibble. I decided to try the runout slough. Green willows, large and small, had grown profusely along the drain during low water. Now they were flooded to a depth of several feet. I waded, using a light cane pole and dropping my worm-baited hook around every likely looking willow or weed clump I could reach. I kept an eye open for the always present cottonmouth; they were likely to be resting on almost any object on or near the water. Less hazardous was the occasional pot hole, but to be avoided if possible. While wading and fishing in four feet of water and intent upon the business at hand. It was very disconcerting to suddenly step into one of these spots a foot or two deeper.

Fishing was good this day, the water was clear and clean looking. There was plenty of cover, nice sunshiny weather, just a few clouds. BUT, no fish! The catching was lousy. After a couple of hours, though, business picked up. I dropped my bait into a thick clump of small submerged willows and ironweed and immediately my small cork floater dived under. I set the hook and, after a spirited fight, landed a feisty drum of about ten inches. He was thick and fat and on the stringer he went. Without moving from the spot I landed twenty-two more of them, from eight to ten inches in length. They were small fish but well-fed and certainly fun to catch. In addition to the drum, I caught a couple of dozen bream. Most of them were long-eared sunfish but several were a variety I'd caught before only in levee ditches and creeks far removed from the river. I'd identified these from my fish identification book as orange-spotted sunfish. I'd caught many of these but never one over four inches in length. They were beautifully colored little fish and, like all sunfish, excellent fighters on light tackle. I released all the bream I caught including the long-ears though they were certainly large enough for pan fish. I culled the drum, keeping a dozen, plus a fat channel cat of a couple pounds. Later, at home, I cleaned these. Mom and Eurith cooked them and they were delicious in a meal which also included black eyed peas, fried okra, sliced tomatoes and cornbread. This was accompanied by iced tea!

After such extended periods of flood time the river was out of its banks for two months. It wasn't unusual to see strange varieties of fish. I frequently saw schools of mullet, many of them cavorting and jumping just as I'd seen mullet do in the Gulf of Mexico. In 1990, during the flood, a huge school of of them moved up the river all the way to the dam. Most fishermen had no idea what they were but quickly found that they would not hit a lure or a hook baited with the usual catfish bait. But someone tried snagging them with a big treble hook and heavy sinker and was quite successful. Most were discarded to die and were wasted but a few were taken home to eat and also many were cut up as catfish or striper bait.

I often have wondered about other salt water species coming up the river. Redfish, Tarpon, and occasionally flounder are known to have an

31

affinity for fresh water. I'm curious about this.

By the summer of 1958, Red River was back in its bed--its usual meandering, lazy self. The lakes were at their low summer level. Most of my fishing for the summer was conducted in Lake Texoma for sandies and schooling black bass; lots of fun, but no sizable fish to speak of. August came and with it my responsibility to return to Guthrie, Oklahoma for another year of teaching. The day before Eurith and I were to leave, John, a former neighbor who now lived in Edmond, stopped by to show me a couple of bass he'd caught. They were real lunkers--one of five pounds and one of six and a half pounds. Earlier that week he had caught a seven pounder. He'd fished in the beer joint lake, wading around the old cedar log and abandoned car bodies. He showed me the lures he liked to use, jointed Pikie type plugs to which he had attached some long white rubber bands. His technique was to reel the plug slowly along the surface and next to the cover, as tight against it as possible.

John left me one of his plugs but I didn't have a chance to fish the beer joint lake until the summer of 1959. Then, I tried the pikie and my old reliable Lucky 13. Good results. Several trips gave me a number of large mouths from two to five pounds.

As time went by the beer joint lake changed a lot, primarily as a result of siltation from the surrounding farmland. The average depth decreased to about three feet with a hole or two possibly of five feet. In the 70's and 80's there were some fish die offs as a result of low water and high temperatures. However, in the cooler months, including springtime, if there had been sufficient high water so as to restock the lake, fishing was pretty good.

Eurith's cousin, Richard, trotlined the lake often in the early 80's and had a lot of success for channel cat. He told me of catching a large number of stripers from schools apparently coming in from the river. Richard also spent a great deal of time catching soft-shell turtles which he had a ready market for. They'd always been plentiful in the river and lake.

Presently, in 2012, the beer joint lake has a dubious status as a fishery. This is also true of Red River itself. Siltation of the big holes from agriculture and gravel and sand operations, plus dairy farm and feed-lot run off have harmed this wonderful ecological system, perhaps fatally.

In its own way Red River and its lakes had much beauty, heavily forested banks, clean water that varied from muddy red to beautiful

32

crystalline depending upon the time of year and rainfall, abundant fish, plentiful wildlife. So much of this has changed.

19 THE GRAPE-VINE CATS

The huge flood of 1957 had the Red River overflowing its banks for several weeks. All of this water meant a huge increase in spawning and feeding area for the river's fish population. There also seemed to be a migration of fish upriver from its lower reaches, and word got out among local fishermen that the river was full of catfish.

My father-in-law, Earl, and Uncle Henry decided to trotline the river for a couple of days. I was invited to go along. We reached the river by going past the Chessir home place, crossing the WPA ditch and driving to the bank of a big backwater "slough" near the mouth of Brown's creek. The slough became part of the river during high-water times, but this time, during late summer, it was open only at the south end since the flood was over and the river had receded into its bed.

The river was a series of large lake-like holes and swift flowing shoals at this time of year. Even within its bed it meandered back and forth with the main body of the stream alternating between the Texas and Oklahoma sides.

Earl and Uncle Henry wanted to fish a huge hole on the Texas side, so we eased a twelve foot jon boat down the slough's bank into the murky water, loaded our tackle and camping gear into the boat, fastened Earl's 5-horsepower motor to the stern, and headed for the mouth of the slough. I rode in the bow or front. My job was to watch for logs embedded in the sandy bottom, and, if we high-centered a sandbar, to pull the boat loose if possible.

We made it from the slough into the river without much trouble and in about 30 minutes had reached our goal--the clean bare sand-bar on the west side on of an enormous, deep, lake-like hole of water. The shoal area we'd come through in the little boat was swift, but the current in the big lake was slow. The "lake" was about a half-mile long, and probably 200 yards or so wide.

We set up camp on the sandbar. Each of us had our own supply of bedding. Mine was pretty compact. In those days, when I camped out I used an army surplus sleeping bag of heavy wool and usually put a single quilt and one pillow in it. This was my bed-roll. I had a change of clothing in it too. It certainly didn't take up much space. Earl and Uncle Henry had similar bedding. We would not be too comfortable, but for a fisherman it'd be OK!

While the two of them set out their lines, I set up camp which was a very simple affair. Our groceries were canned stuff: vienna sausage, potted meat, pork and beans, white bread. We had a 5 gallon can of drinking water and an ice chest with a 25 lb. block of ice for the fish we caught. I dragged firewood from a big drift near the south end of the lake.

The trot-lines were set in the most promising areas of the lake. Earl and Henry each set one line near the place where the swift water entered- one line on each side of the swift water. Henry also set one downstream or north of camp. Earl set another south of camp. He tied the unweighted end to some grape vines that had grown over the limbs of a big cottonwood and, recently, the caving bank had dropped the cottonwood and vines into the river. The vines were full of grapes, some ripening and some still green, but pretty big, about the size of a marble. The other end of the line was tied to a weighted float in the open water.

Though the general direction of flow for Red River is northwest to southeast there are many places where the direction is different because of some quirk in the topography of the area. Just east of the highway 78 bridge the river makes a huge left turn, an enormous sweeping bend, and flows from south to north for several miles before curving back to the east in the vicinity of the mouth of Island Bayou, a tributary. We were fishing in this south to north area.

The guys had baited their lines with a mix of crawfish and yellow grasshoppers. By late afternoon the lines were out and baited, camp was set up and we had a supper of light bread, sliced onions and tomatoes, pork and beans, and vienna sausage. I'd made a pot of fishing coffee, "boiled" in an open can setting on the coals.

They "ran" the trot lines right after supper and didn't have much, just five or six small cats and a couple of gar that were four or five pounds each. We tried seining bait, shad and river shiners, but after several tries only had a couple of dozen. Most of the fishing would have to be done with the crawfish and grasshoppers brought from home.

Earl said, "Let's try some cut bait". So he and I began working on one of the gar. The meat of the gar was white and fine-grained, like crappie. I could see why people would like to eat it.

The lines were rebaited and we settled down by the campfire for a couple of hours of talking, coffee-drinking, and dozing by lantern light.

About ten o'clock Earl and Henry ran their lines and had a surprising number of cats. They were a mixture of channel catfish and humpbacked white catfish, and small blue cats. Most of them were two or three pounders, but a few were smaller. This first run had netted about 25 cats—a pretty good run.

Earl had skipped his grape vine line 'till last. He suggested that he and I check it out while Henry put their catch in the fish box. The fish box was a rectangular affair of heavy wire mesh and steel support rods welded together. If placed in running water, fish in it could survive for several days.

Earl and I started at the open-water end of the line and worked toward the bank. At first the results were just so-so. Not many fish, only four or five for the first twenty hooks. But business picked up as we neared the bank. The second twenty hooks gave another dozen cats, some around five or six pounds. The last seven or eight hooks were deep in the grape vines. The vines still had their leaves as well as fruit and the trotline was tight and hard to pull out. The first hook out had a solid six pounder. Each of the remaining hooks had fish from around four pounds to a real lunker of eight pounds. The grape vines had paid off big time! We brought in twenty-four really nice cats that run.

A couple of hours later Earl and I ran his lines again. His line near the swifter water gave up only seven catfish of one to two pounds each, but also a fat paddlefish of fifteen pounds snagged in the grapevine. The grapevine yielded another big catch, another fifteen fish up to five pounds!

The next morning Earl and Henry decided they'd better take the fish in since they had such a big amount. While they cleaned the fish, I broke camp putting things away as compactly as possible. I left breakfast supplies out. We'd cook and eat after the fish cleaning.

"Come look at this," said Earl as he held up the innards of a large catfish he was cleaning. The belly of the fish was filled with grapes,

35

some green, others ripe! Many of the other cats also had obviously grazed among the vines. Catfish are that way about food. And so were we. After a big breakfast of bacon, fried eggs, light bread soaked with Uncle Henry's favorite gravy (straight bacon grease), and strong fisherman's coffee, we headed home with almost a hundred pounds of cleaned catfish iced down. We had to make two trips to the car because of such a load!

20 BIG FISH IN THE BIG HOLE

In 1958 my cousin Carl and I decided to return to the grape vine hole where we caught the big catfish for a day's fishing. We parked on the tall bank by the slough, and each carried a rod and a tackle bag containing lunch, lures, and stringer, down the trail to the water's edge and waded the shallow end. We'd walk the sandy beach to the big hole on the Texas side.

Usually, for our river fishing, we carried hooks and sinkers as well as lures. In addition, we ordinarily took a seine or some jugging jars for catching bait. The jugs had some advantages, three or four of them plus a bag of oatmeal for bait and placed in a tow-sack were much more compact and easier to carry than a wet,' sandy seine. In addition, they were about as efficient for bait catching. But, on this particular day, we took only lures since we'd decided to fish the swift water for sandies and around the drifts for black bass. Our choice of lures varied according to our individual desires. I had an assortment of spoons plus a couple of Tiny Lucky 13's. Carl preferred Shyster spinners and Baby Hula poppers. My rod was a five foot solid glass, medium action True Temper, the reel was a Zebco close-faced spin-caster loaded with twelve pound line. Carl's tackle was similar; close-faced Zebco on a light five or five and a half foot rod. These were our standard river fishing outfits and they did a good job on the small to medium-sized fish we usually caught. I preferred level wind bait casters for some fishing, but on the river they usually became sanded and useless. Zebcos weren't so easily damaged. The walk across the beach took a while, about half an hour or so. This beach area is terrific wildlife habitat. Great numbers of salt-cedar and willows furnish cover and there is a variety of seed producers: lespedeza, Johnston grass, partridge peas, and in some areas, goatweed. In the less sandy areas there were blackberry vines and persimmons and grapes. Quail, doves, rabbits, and rarely deer are found here at times. So are coyotes and bobcats. The closer one gets to the water, the more sparse the vegetation becomes. The edge of the river is pretty bare.

As we walked up to the edge of the big hole I saw a fish strike into some bait about thirty feet from the shore. "Make a cast", Carl said. I snapped a Johnson Silver minnow on to my line, hooked on a medium length of white, wiggly pork rind and flipped the bait into the circular disturbance caused by the striking fish. Immediately I had a savage strike and a sizable fish was on. Its identity was quickly revealed as it jumped several times in an attempt to shake the bait loose. Carefully, I played and landed a spotted bass which pulled the De-liar to the three pound mark.

I strung the fish and, encouraged, we began working the white, wiggly pork rind and flipped the bait into the circular disturbance caused by the striking fish. Immediately I had a savage strike and a sizable fish was on. Its identity was quickly revealed as it jumped several times in an attempt to shake the bait loose. Carefully, I played and landed a spotted bass which pulled the De-liar to the three pound mark. I strung the fish and, we began working the deeper water of the hole in earnest. No additional strikes.

The big hole had changed a bit since the cat fishing trip a year earlier. Most of the swift water flow now entered at the south end instead of the middle as a result of the meandering of the river in its bed. The original swift channel was now a shallow, easily waded riffle. The main channel at the south end had brought in some logs. These had snagged and haphazardly sanded in. They were washed by clear, clean-looking water. We figured this would be a good area to try, and so we headed that way. As we walked along I noticed that the big cottonwood covered with grape vines where Earl had caught so many catfish had toppled off the undercut bank. The vines, minus their foliage, were still attached. It looked to be a terrific place to try, in a boat!

When we reached the log-drift we found the river had narrowed enough to enable us to cast across to the logs. Carl made the first cast while I was tying out my bass. "I've got one," he said, "and it's a good one." He played in a whopper sand bass of two pounds which had smashed his Shyster spinner.

We went to work seriously at that point and after an hour's fishing had strung a dozen nice sandies and four channel cat of about a pound each.

The channels hit the Shyster and a Weber spoon colored like a shad. Finally, the fishing at the drift tapered off and our results for a couple of hours were sixteen sandies, most pan-sized, but a couple of two pounders, and six cats including one of two and one-half pounds. We'd lost three or four lures each to the snags.

We decided to move farther down the big hole and give it a try, but first we ate our pork and beans, viennas, and light bread. We each had a good cold drink from the thermos.

We divided our load, one of us carrying tackle, the other carrying the heavy stringer of fish. We waded the shallow riffle and decided to try the mid-section of the hole again.

My first cast into the deep, relatively still water resulted in a heavy strike. For a moment I had a big fish on but then, nothing! Upon reeling in I found that my line had been neatly clipped in two. Carl had a similar result.

We tied back on from our dwindling supply of lures. I selected a yellow spoon with black polka dots. After a few casts, an enormous fish hit the spoon and took off downstream. There wasn't much I could do but hold on and try to keep a good bend in the rod! Finally, the fish slowed and I began gaining line. Slowly, I managed to work him back. At last we were able to get a good look at him in the clear water. A big catfish, blue or channel, had hit the spoon. We estimated his weight at fifteen or twenty pounds. But I was not to touch him, we reached an impasse, I couldn't move him any closer with my light tackle in the swift current and finally he made another run and pulled loose.

We continued casting. We each tied into another monster. Again, our lines were cut and our lures lost. Carl eventually fought another big one in close enough for us to identify it in the clear water. Before it clipped his line we could see what our adversaries were huge garfish at least forty pounds, some perhaps bigger. The odds of landing one on light tackle and twelve pound line were, to say the least, pretty low. But we tried! We had a ball, hanging and then losing those big ones!

I tied on my last lure, a white spoon with black spots and made a hard cast. My lure sailed out about forty feet and stopped, kerplunking into the water! I tried another, same results. Thinking I had a line snazzle inside my reel I removed the cover for inspection. No snazzle but no line either, at least not much. Of the full spool I had at the beginning of the day only about fifteen yards remained. I was also left with only one spoon of the dozen or so I'd started with.

Carl's tackle was similarly depleted. We gathered up our tackle and a heavy stringer of sandies and small cats and headed home. We'd had a day of fighting some monsters, and lost! But terrific fun!

21 FLY FISHING

In 1932, my Dad and another teacher, Mr. Corley, went to Little River for a couple of days to camp and fish. Mr. Corley had fished the eastern rivers of Oklahoma for several years. These rivers are Little, Glover, and Mountain Fork. They are all tributaries of the Red, but, unlike Red are rock-bottomed clear water streams. They all have nice tributary creeks which may be excellent fishing also. They have a varied assortment of fish. The top game fish is probably the smallmouth bass, but largemouth are also plentiful. Others include goggle-eyes, which are the species known as green sunfish, long-ear sunfish, bluegill, channel cat, flathead cat, drum, and several kinds of gar. Kentucky spotted bass were abundant also.

Mr. Corley was a fly fisherman and had used this system enough to be very adept at it. Dad had never fly fished but intended to use a cane pole and minnows which the two of them would seine from the river backwaters.

The river was clear and the fishing was good. Mr. Corley caught a limit of bass and a stringer full of goggle-eye each day. Dad's fishing was not so productive, but nevertheless he caught several nice ones.

Mr. Corley talked him into trying the fly rod. Dad reluctantly agreed and was able to land several nice ones. He even tried casting a fly with his cane pole and had some success.

By the next fishing season Dad has acquired his own fly fishing tackle. His rod was a ten dollar split bamboo, and his reel was a small, light, dollar and a half one. Rod, reel, and fly line were all from Montgomery Ward through their mail order catalog. The twelve dollars he'd spent on this tackle were quite an expenditure, but he figured it'd be worth it because of the fresh fish he'd bring home.

Dad and my mother's brothers fished these mountain streams infrequently through the years of the Great Depression. My uncles eventually acquired their own fly fishing tackle and it became their favorite method of fishing. World War II interrupted these trips to the streams, however.

After the war when rationing of gasoline was over, trips to the rivers resumed. Fishing was good and the boys generally enjoyed several such fishing/camping trips each summer. They expanded their range to include the Cossatot and Saline rivers in southwestern Arkansas. They began taking their families on their trips quite often. As a boy of ten or twelve years I enjoyed this immensely: The place where we lived, upon moving from Albany to Yuba in 1942, had unlimited possibilities for a young lad who loved the outdoors. With the house came over a hundred acres of "pastureland" but it was mostly heavily wooded. A nice creek wandered through it, fed by several smaller branches. The creek was only about fifty yards back of our house. It had just about everything that could be desired in such a small, lowland creek. Clear, clean water, except after heavy rains which muddied it, gravel beds, drifts, and best of all, in these years of the 1940's,it was free of trash and was unpolluted.

During those years, if not in school, my waking hours were spent outdoors. There was gardening, mowing, and taking care of our livestock which included chickens, guineas, pigs, a milk cow and calf, and many chores related to these critters. But I always found time to fish in the creek, or squirrel hunt, or simply roam the woods. This was the perfect home for a boy as crazy about the outdoors as I was: I'll never forget those happy times or the lessons I learned in this environment.

The creek back of our house was a branch of Brown's Creek. Since Brown's Creek drained into the Red, it and its tributaries generally had an abundant population of fish. The species present usually included green sunfish. These were called goggle-eye or black perch. They were fierce little predators and quite often reached a decent size of a solid half pound and eight inches in length. There were some monsters of this species which were even larger! Other species present included long-ears, which appeared different from those in the mountain streams, an occasional bluegill, a rare bass or crappie, creek cats or bull heads, an assortment of different kinds of minnows and shiners, and very rarely, gar and suckers.

I helped keep our family fed with squirrels from the woods and fish from the creek. The goggle-eyes were our favorites, but the little creek cats were delicious too and always were welcome. Getting bait was as simple as turning a shovel of soil in the place where I emptied the kitchen slop bucket.

The soil was loaded with red worms and grubs. I also used grasshoppers which were always available in the summer, but red worms were the best.

Here, in this creek at home, I learned to fly fish. There were good-sized potholes in the creek separated by swift running shoals with bright, clean water running over gravel beds. The potholes were fairly deep, some of them as much as twenty or more feet long and about half as wide.

Dad didn't fish the creek very often, and when he did he used his fly rod and small popping bugs, I fished it almost every day, or swam in it, or simply roamed its banks to discover what I could about it.

I learned to swim, teaching myself, when I was around nine years old. I'd been warned to stay out of the deeper holes, but one day while trying to catch the red crawfish that lived by the hundreds in the creek, I suddenly found myself in water deeper than I was tall. Frantically, I splashed and paddled, scared even more witless than I usually was! All at once, I found it: something I have never lost. I could swim! I simply swam across the hole, then back. I tried some of the other holes, even the big round hole down near the highway. It worked in every pot-hole in the creek. I could swim!

My boyhood friend and partner in crime, Gerald, and I had a world of new opportunities after this. We swam every hole big enough in the creek and its branches. Each winter we could hardly wait for the swimming season, which, surely as everyone knew began on March 1. Even if a little ice had to be broken in order to reach the water:

One spring morning Dad said," Get the minnow bucket, son". Let's fish the creek a little, And bring my fly rod." We kept our tackle, including my light cane poles for bait fishing, in the old smoke house by our main house. No longer used as a smoker it was a good storage building for tackle, dad's carpentry tools, the lawn mower, mom's boxes of fruit jars for canning, and any other items we wanted to keep out of the weather and separate from our living quarters.

We walked down the creek toward the Highway 78 bridge about a quarter of a mile from the house. Just above this small bridge was the biggest hole in the creek. It was a good forty feet wide, was almost perfectly round and seven or eight feet deep at this time. A long. gravel shoal from our branch led into it and another branch, from the south, also fed it. During the heavy spring rains each year water from these two branches joined at this point and the resulting maelstrom had gouged out this hole and kept it open each year. The main part of this round hole was off to the side of the creek channel in normal water conditions, and so the hole was like a pond. The creek ran under Highway 78, east for half a mile, then south for about three quarters of a mile joining Brown's Creek which cut through the old Grassy Lake bed. Brown's Creek had many branches, all containing a variety of fish in those days.

Dad flicked his fly rod, flipping a little white popper with rubber bands legs and painted-on eyes, into the first hole east of the bridge. The water was clear and clean. It was full of minnows and bugs. Whammo! A fish smacked the popper. Dad played him carefully--a fat goggle eye bigger than one's hand, an honest three-quarter pounder, almost black in the shaded creek water. Into the minnow bucket he went. We were after a mess of fish. We worked our way east, trying each hole, catching fish almost constantly. Some were long ears, some blue gill bream, and there were a few small bass. We released everything but the goggle eyes. Dad insisting that it was time for me to learn to fly fish handed me the rod. We couldn't really cast because of the closeness of willows and button bushes to the creek and so we just flipped the little popper into each hole. No matter, it worked as well as you'd want it. We tried a yellow popper. It was just as effective. Goggle eyed perch are fierce fighters on light tackle and prodigious eaters of bugs!

We began releasing all our fish as we caught them. Finally, we were tired. We'd had a great morning of fishing our home creek. The minnow bucket was full of the black perch. Later, back at the house, we cleaned twenty-one of them, of an almost uniform size averaging about eight or nine inches and close to three quarters of a pound. We had enough for a couple of good meals. An unforgettable day for me!

About a week later, I flipped a yellow popper into a small, deep hole just back of our house. A savage, wicked strike! I'd never had a fish on, this size, from our creek. An enormous goggle eye, twelve and a half inches long, just an ounce or so less than two pounds on my Christmas present De-Liar. I've never seen another this large after over half a century of fishing, and countless trips to Oklahoma's eastern rivers. It was a real giant of its kind.

22 THE WILD RIVERS

After World War II, Shakespeare began making tubular fiber- glass rods. Uncle Fate bought a ten foot, three piece rod which he used until his death in 1966. Dad and my other uncles each obtained similar tackle. Dad's preference was for a lighter two piece eight and a half footer. I inherited his bamboo rod, which by now was beginning to show signs of age. The varnish finish was beginning to crack, the guides were grooved and both tip sections had been snapped resulting in a decrease of about four inches off the original length of eight feet. With Dad's help, I replaced the guides and put a new tip-top on each tip section. The bamboo by now was getting pretty brittle. Never one of the expensive, top of the line rods, it was showing the effects of fifteen years of pretty heavy usage. My fly reel was about shot, too. It was dented, rusty, and the brake ratchet was worn out. Nevertheless, I was high as a kite! I had my own fly rod.

During the summer of 1947 through 1952 we made a number of fishing trips to Little River and Glover. We camped at the mouth of Cloudy Creek on Little River and when we went to Glover we usually camped on the old Jones Ranch road near an old flood- destroyed bridge. This was wild country in those days. The Dierk's, lumber company was the landowner and they left it open for public access.

If ever an industrial company followed practices good for wildlife and the environment, Dierk's had to be the one. There was no clear cutting, the hardwoods were not eradicated, there was no siltation of the streams, no poisons. Just air as clean as a person can breathe and creeks and rivers you can drink from. We didn't carry drinking water on our camping trips to these rivers--just ice, and we'd carry water from the river to camp. When fishing, if one became thirsty, just drink from the creek!

I did this hundreds of times. Small tributary creeks running into Glover and Mountain Fork were crystal clear and some were icy cold. The fish in these little creeks were of types, different than those in the main river and larger creeks.

Little River, being closer to civilization, was more heavily fished. But in those days it was still a good fishing stream. Access was good because the roads and bridges were well maintained.

Our favorite was Glover--more remote, just getting there was an adventure. Our trips to Glover usually lasted from three days to a week and so we'd carry a lot of groceries and much ice which we purchased in Antlers. The ice was in fifty pound blocks. We'd obtain three or four blocks for a week's fishing. Wrapped in old quilts and then tarps they'd last for the whole trip with a lot to spare. One block was designated for iced tea and cold drinking water, the others for storing fresh meats and fruits and vegetables and the fish we'd keep take home. I do not recall ever losing any fresh food, including fish, on any of these trips we made. Ice chests were taken, if room was available and ice, chipped from these blocks was often added to keep the contents of the chests cold. Take home fish usually was stored in these.

Mountain Fork river was the most remote of the streams we fished. Our camp ground was located north of Broken Bow in a spot that, in those days, bordered on being inaccessible. Our usual plan for a trip to this area was to take supplies sufficient for a week and to leave all the regular cars at a little community called Bethel. We'd load all our gear into pick-up trucks for the drive from Bethel to the river, a distance of about twelve miles. The access road was one of the old Dierks logging roads and generally was in terrible condition. There were only couple of lesser turn-off roads that appeared to be usable. They probably led to cabins which were inhabited by people trying to make a living by hunting and fishing and farming the small meadow fields scattered through the piney woods.

In June of 1951, we made such a trip. "We" included my uncles, Fate, Rob, Frank, and George, my mother's brothers, and my Dad and I. In addition, a couple of their old fishing cronies, somewhat related as distant cousins, went along. Uncle George's friend Lloyd came down from Oklahoma City. He drove a big, old army surplus truck which would be used to transport us and the camping gear from Bethel into the river. We met at Uncle Rob's place, east of Durant, loaded most of the camping gear and supplies into the truck, and set off early on a beautiful spring morning. The journey to Bethel would take about three and a half hours.

We stopped at Broken Bow to purchase ice and groceries, then on to Bethel we headed. About midway between Broken Bow and Bethel there was a roadside park area where we stopped for lunch.

The park was beautiful and primitive. There were hickory, oak, and pine trees and a lawn like grassy area that the highway workers mowed.

Only a couple of concrete picnic tables were present, but since, in those days, the roads were lightly traveled by anyone other than loggers, they were enough. I was fascinated by an open spring bubbling out of the ground a short distance from the tables. A small pit had been dug as a receptacle and was lined with rocks from the bed of the tiny stream that drained the spring water into a larger creek. A sign, posted near the spring indicated that this was a natural drinking water source and requested that users please keep it clean and free of any debris or food scraps. The water looked pure and was crystal clear. We used coffee cups and each had a drink. The water was ice cold and perfect:

Lloyd had brought with him several big four pound sticks of summer sausage. We cut thin slices from one and opened a loaf of bread. Someone peeled a red onion, another opened a couple of cans of pork and beans. These, along with sharp "rat" cheese, made up our lunch.

The owner of the general store at Bethel was an acquaintance of Dad and the uncles. He'd grown up in Bryan County and they'd known each other from their ball-playing days. He was glad to see us and after a round of cold pop and candy bars and a short visit, we parked our car and Uncle Frank's pickup alongside the store, loaded the rest of the gear into Lloyd's truck and set off for the river. Uncle Fate drove his pick-up in so we'd have an extra vehicle in case of emergency.

The trip in to the camp ground was relatively smooth, considering the quality of the road. The only incident of note was a delay to watch a group of deer, four adults and two fawns, browsing in a clearing around an old abandoned sawmill.

When we arrived at the camp ground, the left front tire on the big truck was gasping its last. Lloyd had said that his tires weren't any good and this one had given way to the sharp rocks it had encountered. Fortunately, he was able to park the truck in a handy spot for camping. He'd brought three spares, anticipating problems such as this. We'd exchange the flat tire for a spare at our leisure sometime during the five day trip.

Our camp ground was a large one. It had enough space for another group, if needed. No other campers ever showed up to share it, though, and none ever did in the many trips we made over the years. The camp area was a fairly good-sized clearing alongside the old logging road that we'd followed in. Another, even more primitive, worn out road from the north joined our road at the east side of camp.

45

A cold, clear spring branch flowed alongside our road and would supply water for drinking, cooking and washing dishes. We were careful not to contaminate this branch. Our hand washing and fish cleaning would be done several yards below our drinking water source. Bathing would be done in the river.

The river was about seventy yards east of camp. A large, deep hole was backed by a steep mountain which came right down to the water's edge. Because of this barrier the original builders of the road, the Dierk's lumber company, had turned off to the right or south and then forded the river at a rocky shoal below the big hole. The road, upon emerging from the river, on its east side, spiraled around the sides of a lower mountain and then headed farther east.

The hills and mountains of this area were heavily wooded during these years. Hardwoods, such as hickory, several species of oak, ash, beech, and gum, in addition to the ever present pine and varied shrubbing comprised the forest. Along the river and its creeks bald cypress was common and at the confluence of the creeks and the river in deeper richer topsoil there were mulberry, blackberry, and chinquapin or wild filbert. Wild blueberries or huckleberries were common in clearings.

Narrow gauge railways or tramways were scattered in segments through the forest. These were ancient, falling apart, and no longer usable. They had been constructed during the years in which horse or mule-drawn heavy duty wagons were used to pick up pine logs. The trams received the logs from an area, then delivered then to a more centralized collection point from which trucks would transport then to the Dierk's sawmill. These tramways had the effect of narrow clearings in the heavy forest. They naturally grew up in berry vines and so were a great place to "pick a pie" or perhaps shoot a squirrel or two.

Uncle Fate always brought a .22 rifle on these trips. The gun was used for squirrels around the mulberry trees in the creek bottoms, or for killing the occasional rattler or copperhead that made its way to camp.

Mainly, we planned to fly fish on these trips. If the water was off-colored as it sometimes was after heavy showers we'd seine minnows and, using cane poles we'd brought, wade fish. The style was to flip the line out in front, dabbling the bait around larger rocks which give the fish a break from the swift current. Any structure such as a sanded-in snag, log, patch of weeds, or lily pads, was fished thoroughly. The snags, pads, and weeds generally were in areas away from the main current. Usually, in the larger holes, there were plenty of logs and brush piles. The water in such holes, however, was generally too deep for wading and frequently had inaccessible banks, and so were ignored by us except for the few times a boat was brought along. The rigging for cane pole fishing with live bait involved a ten to twelve foot pole. The running line was a length of braided nylon casting line, usually black, fastened near the butt end of the pole. A few feet of line was tied with a series of half-hitches to the small end, several feet of line was wrapped around the end and then three or more half-hitches to secure it. A length equal to about the length of the pole was allowed to hang free from the tip. A loop was tied at the end of this length. If a floater was desired the line was passed through the hole in the cork. Whether or not a floater was used, the loop then was interlocked with the loop in the leader of a small, stout, snelled hook. Usually for bass, goggle eye, or channel cat a size 1 or l/0 hook was used. A clinch-on sinker was placed on the line just above the leader. For bait, river shiners were best, but difficult to catch and more difficult to keep alive. Crawfish from the river itself or tributaries were very desirable. Earthworms from home worked well on cats and the assortment of sunfish or perch as we called them.

But the main thing, our primary objective, was always to use the fly rod. We used only two or three different kinds of flies. Our favorites were popping bugs, either yellow or white. They were made of painted cork, eyes painted on, white rubber band legs and tail feathers over the hook. We used size 4 or 6 for most fishing. If we saw evidence of bigger fish we'd change. to a size 2 or size 1 bug. These were too large for most of the fish we encountered.

Most of the rods were eight and a half footers, with the exception being Uncle Fate's ten foot wonder-rod. Our reels were simple, single action devices, dragless but with a brake which was used mainly to maintain line tension when the fly was in the hook keeper. This brake rather quickly became useless because the ratchet mechanism was weak. These reels were used only for holding line, not for fighting the bass or pan fish we usually caught. They were light and comfortable, and durable but eventually had to be replaced. No problem there because a perfectly usable fly reel could be purchased for $1.50 to $2.00. Dad and I tried the spring operated reels of Shakespeare and South-Bend but gave up on them after about a season of use. The springs, upon wearing, either were too weak and refused to draw in line or sometimes the reel would become super automatic and zip the lines in without the lever being activated. After several dissections and regroupings of these reels we finally gave up and into the waste basket they went and we came back to our old single-actions. They weren't really multipliers for each turn of the handle only one revolution of the spool was made.

A couple of years after this trip, Dad's friend who had a sporting goods store in Durant offered him a couple of Pfleuger Progress reel, which normally cost around four dollars, for half-price. At this present date, over sixty years later, I still have mine, as good as new after catching thousands of bass and pan fish.

The lines we used were level. We knew nothing of tapered lines. They weren't even available in our area. These lines had a finish that gradually became sticky with use and so about twice each season I stripped the line from the reels and washed them with soap and warm water. We replaced them about every two years as the finish wore off. Obviously, our reels and lines were inexpensive, even cheap. But of necessity!

We used no backing; none was needed for our style of fishing. Leaders were cat-gut when Dad first started fly fishing. After the war, when I began with the fly rod he still had several spools of this material which I didn't like, it was thick, brittle, and hard to tie. By the late 40's, monofilament leader material became available and was much better.

I'm sure our leaders and, in fact, all our fly fishing equipment would be a shock to the average fly fisherman of today. We had no tapered leaders, just level monofilament. Our average leader was probably no more than two feet long. My Uncle Frank refused to use a leader more than a foot in length or testing less than twenty pounds. Once, when I made up a four foot leader of five pound material he and my dad laughed and said it would never work. But it did!

Besides popping bugs we mostly used just two other flies. One of these was a feather job, probably maribou, colored black and with the mandatory rubber band legs. It had a thin strip of aluminum foil running down the back and logically became known as the "silver streak". We fished these bare, sometimes, but more often added a paper-thin, white, strip of Uncle Josh fly rind to the hook. To increase the rind's action we'd carefully split it from the tail to the hook hole. This arrangement looked as enticing as a hot-hipped hula dancer: The seductive qualities of this lure were

48

enhanced, we thought, by fastening a tiny Hildebrand spinner to the eye of the hook. This lure, spinner, fly, and rind was wretched to cast but at times was deadly on small-mouth bass and big goggle-eyes.

Another fly we used, but less often, was called the guinea fly. It was somewhat similar to the "silver streak" but had a guinea feather tied over the back of the hook. We also, in later years, used rubber bugs which had a tuft of gray and white buck-tail tied to the hook eyes and the hair projected past the curved part of the hook shank. We sometimes referred to this latter type as "the skunk fly".

As I grew older, I experimented with others. One of these was a honey bee patterned wet fly which I discovered was known as the McGinty. I used it with a very thin strip of split fly rind and found it to be deadly for goggle-eyes and long-ears but not so good for bass. I also tried the black gnat as did some of my uncles but with indifferent results.

When traveling to our fishing-camping spot on any of the three rivers, Little, Glover, or Mountain Fork, we almost always drove through the little town of Antlers. It became traditional for us to buy camping supplies at a Piggly Wiggly store just east of town. Another reason we chose the Antlers route was the presence of a couple of stores, one being Oklahoma Tire and Supply, the other was Babcock Brothers. They were on the same city block and only a couple of doors apart. We purchased our fishing supplies, mainly flies, at these two stores. Usually, each of us would leave with eight to twelve of the flies knowing that if the fishing was good we'd "wear out" several of the bugs.

It was, for me, a real treat to do this for I had my own money since I worked around my home community of Yuba each summer doing farm work of various kinds, saving money for school clothes, but spending a lot of it for tackle and fishing magazines:

"Let's go down river", Uncle Fate said early the morning of the first full day of this latest trip. I knew he had in mind a specific hole we had fished several times before with good results. And so we set off just after breakfast, the air so cool, clean and fresh, trees dripping their nights' dew. The woods would heat up after a few hours of sunshine but now they were like a long, cold, drink of water to a parched dusty traveler.

We followed the old road paralleling the river for about a half mile to the ford, crossed the river and then picked up a game trail heading more or less in the direction we wanted. After around twenty more minutes or so we left the trail turning off to the right and the river. We hit the river in a shoaling area at the downstream end of a long pond-like body of water with almost imperceptible current. A brisk, whitewater rapids rushed from this almost still pool into a smaller deep pool about thirty yards wide. Though the pool was deep the tops of a couple of huge boulders were visible near the center of it.

This was our main destination. We'd fish it thoroughly before moving on and trying the next shoal. These shoals, though shallow, usually held lots of fish. They were littered with irregular outcroppings and small boulders around which one could expect to find smallmouth and black perch.

We limbered up our casting arms at the tail end of the big hole using popping bugs and stringing a couple of the goggle-eyes each while releasing a half dozen longears too small to keep. My uncle said "I have a bass". And I watched him play and release a smallie of around ten inches. In our camp we had an informal rule that small-mouths shorter than twelve inches were to be released.

We moved carefully past the rapids, uncle taking the east bank. I waded to shore, skirted a clump of willows and started to almost step on a big water snake lying in the edge of the stream and swallowing his breakfast, a frog still struggling against his destiny. I re-entered the river on the west side, loosed my fly from the keeper and whipped it toward some submerged rocks just below the rapids. "Whack" - as a smallie of about eleven inches hit it. I played and released the bass and cast again to that area. The bass were stacked in the oxygenated water at the base of the rapids and were striking into a school of river shiners. I released four more before tiring of the small ones and began looking for something larger.

I worked my way around the pool toward its south end and the next shoal. No results. I snipped off the yellow popper and tied on a number four silver streak with a spinner and rind, but still no action around the rocks rimming the pool.

Uncle Fate, on the shady side of the river was doing better. He'd strung three nice goggle-eyes and released a half dozen small bass including two large mouths.

I decided to try the deep-water boulders whose tops I could just see. Moving into waist-deep water I cast toward the nearest of the big rocks. I let the silver streak sink for a few seconds, then began slowly stripping it. I felt a slight, tentative touch, set my hook - but nothing!

I tried the farthest boulder. No result. Repeated a half-dozen casts. Disheartened, I decided to move on but decided on one more cast to the first boulder. I moved into deeper water so as to be able to cast between the two. I worked the fly past the place where I'd had two bumps. Now I was in chest-water and had to stand on tip-toes to reach the spot I wanted to cast to. Again, I allowed the fly to sink, and then stripped it slowly. As the lure reached the nearest of the rocks I felt a resistance. Instinctively, I set the hook. My line angled down toward the base of the boulder. "Hung up" I said disgustedly to myself as I failed to budge whatever I'd contacted.

Suddenly, my line angled upward. I could hardly believe what happened next! A huge smallmouth leaped two feet above the water, red eyes blazing, gills flaring, brown body, with vertical bars curling in the sun's rays filtering through the pine and sweet-gum on the east bank.

Mouth agape, all I knew was to hold on. "My God , you have a big bass," my uncle yelled. "Play him carefully, don't hurry things, keep your rod bent!" Yeah! I tried to follow his advice. The fish jumped twice more, luckily he stayed stuck. He settled down into an under-water fight to reach the rocky bottom where he could scratch my fly from his jaw. I kept as much tension on him as I dared. The tip of my old bamboo rod finally gave way from the taped wrapping I'd repaired it with. It slid down the line, trailing the blue repair tape, and toward the fish. I was now simply standing in the pool, in waist-deep water, turning so as to keep up with the circular path the bass was traveling around me. At last I was able to work him close enough to grasp his lower jaw. We were both totally exhausted. Fastening him to my stringer I slogged toward a nearby rock in the shallows and sat down to rest and repair my tackle as best I could. "Good work", my uncle said. Later, at camp the bass measured twenty-two inches and hit five pounds on my De-Liar.

In the years since, I've never caught a more satisfying fish of any species. My regret now is that I didn't release this fierce, beautiful fighter. A few days after returning home from this trip, I awoke one morning to find an elongated, round blue-colored box propped against my bed. A card dangled by a length of fishing of fishing line from it. "Happy fishing, son", was the message on the card. I opened the blue tube and found my first really good fly-rod - a seven foot, nine inch Wonder rod. I used it until 1977, when it was replaced by a Fenwick - eight footer. The old bamboo, repaired so often finally gave up the ghost. The tip section had been snapped several times and the resulting shortness had stiffened it so much that it was almost que-stick like in action. The glue binding the strips together, was giving way. Sadly I retired it to the smoke-house. We never used it again.

23 A VISITOR

The first night of this Mountain Fork trip, we had a supper of Aunt Ola's smothered chicken which she'd cooked and packed in Uncle Rob's big dutch oven, along with a big pan of potatoes. I was washing dishes, Dad and the uncles had spread a quilt to settle down to their customary nightly games of pitch, when we heard a clattering noise down river in the direction of the ford.

"Sounds like some one's coming" dad said. Uncle Fate arose from the quilt pallet, walked over to his pickup and leaned against the door. Inside the open window and propped butt down, muzzle to the roof was his .22 rifle. He always made sure that the gun was readily accessible for any emergency. As the source of the noise neared camp we heard a male voice "Gee," "Haw", with reference to two names - Mandy and Bill. Finally an apparition came into view, came right up the road alongside camp. When we saw what it was we relaxed -- sort of!

A pair of big mules we assumed to be Mandy and Bill was pulling a big wagon. A young man, thirtyish, was atop the driver's seat, holding the reins or lines. "Whoa, mules," he said and the pair stopped in their tracks. "How're ya'll doing?" he said. Uncle Frank explained that we were camping for a while and intended to do some fishing. The young fellow, friendly enough, told us that he lived in a cabin on one of the turn off roads a couple of miles farther toward Bethel. He said "I have a field, about seven acres, on the other side of the river, past that big mountain. "It's a couple of miles from here". He went on to explain that he grew sweet-corn and other truck for market and the sweet-corn was ready now, watermelons and sweet-potatoes come off later. "I'll haul this load out to Bethel tomorrow morning and come back in for another, early day after tomorrow. It takes half a day for me to pick a full load. I'm by myself and hand-pick it all. I have a wife and two kids at our cabin. "This is how I make a living - along with fishing and hunting. I also trap coons and possums and sometimes mink in the winter," he said. His wagon was customized for the kind of work - high sideboards, so as to carry a big load, a lantern board solidly fastened inside the wagon and from which a big lantern hung. Another lantern sat by the driver's seat along with two or three jugs which may have contained white gas for the lantern or as we discussed later, may have been filled with another "white" liquid – white lightning from corn distillate! This wagon was filled with the green sweet-corn. The load was obviously a heavy one. What appeared to be an ancient single- shot shotgun nestled by the driver's seat away from the lantern and almost out of sight.

Uncle Rob came over and said that we'd be here about a week, and if the young man wanted we'd trade him some fish for some sweet corn. The young fellow seemed to relax and smiled that would be fine - help yourself now. Rob said "We'll take a few ears tonight and then when you come Wednesday we'll have a mess of fish for you." The barter completed to the satisfaction of both parties, our visitor departed - "geeing and hawing" to Mandy and Bill until out of sight and sound. Our group seemed almost speechless for a while until Uncle Rob spoke up "Kelwyn, let's shuck the corn and get it on ice."

The rest of that trip we had all the corn we wanted to eat - we boiled it, roasted it, in the shuck, in our campfire coals, and even cut some from the cob and fried it in the bacon grease with diced up onion. This was my favorite.

The young man returned to our camp several times during that week. We never exchanged names but everyone involved were friendly. Each time we had a good mess of fish for him and in return, he supplied us with all the sweet corn we could eat.

The following year, 1952, we returned again in June. And again made acquaintance with our young friend. He seemed glad to see us, said that he was still farming his patch back of the big mountain. He was having problems with deer eating his crops, and had been forced to shoot a couple of them. Of course, he couldn't let the meat go to waste. In order to supplement his income he was cutting short logs for pulp-wood a couple of days per week.

We returned to the Mountain Fork camp in 1953 but didn't see him. After that, for a variety of reasons, including the deaths of Uncle Rob and Uncle George. We confined our wild-river trips to Little River and Glover, finally returning to Mountain Fork in 1959.

We took two pick-ups for that trip. Uncles Fate and Frank, Frank Jr. Freeman, an uncle in-law, and my cousin Doug went along on this one. We drove the heavily-loaded pick-ups along the same road that had served us before for many other trips. The drive from Bethel was a tough one. No sort of maintenance had been done on the road in our absence. It was almost impassable. We were forced to stop a number of times to cut saplings of pine and sweet gum from the road way in order to move on. The ruts, as one would expect had deteriorated into chug holes and miniature drainage ditches. We had to stop once and shoo a mama raccoon and her twins from the roadway. They were so unafraid of us that cousin Doug picked up the young ones and brought over to nine-year old Frank Jr. to see. Mamma coon didn't care for this and Doug rather quickly returned them.

The turn-off road to our farmer friend's cabin was almost obscured by weeds and brush, indicating a lack of human inhabitants for several years. Only a memory of this young fellow remained. We never even knew his name.

We went down on a Monday, left for home early Thursday morning; fishing two full days. Uncles Fate and Frank fished together, concentrating on the holes within easy walking distance of camp. Doug and his dad, Freeman, fished the big hole by camp. They had rigged a couple of inner tubes with straps so they could float-fish that hole. They had pretty good results using red worms and crawfish brought from home. They also were the guardians of Frank Jr. when his dad was on the river.

I fished below camp. I never went as far down river as the hole in which I'd caught the giant smallmouth but spent my time on the shoals and holes just past the old ford. I had good success for the two days, around three dozen black perch and long-ears, a number of releasable size smallies and a surprising number of keeper-size ones with a smattering of largemouth's and spots. I caught fifteen of the bigger bass, ranging from fourteen to seventeen inches releasing most but keeping enough of them plus some of the bigger goggle-eyes for a good mess of fish each day.

Over the years I'd come to appreciate the advantages of fine tackle—longer, lighter leaders and better knots. I rigged, for the first day, a six foot leader of six pound test and brought in a big stringer. The second day I used a four pound test leader and again had excellent results - except once! While fishing my way along I saw a large bass strike a minnow or small sunfish. He was a dandy! Cautiously, I approached the spot. I could now see

54

a large rock from which the bass probably had ambushed his prey. I flicked the yellow Long John popper across current, just upstream from the rock. I let the current gently move the popper down to what I felt was the hot-spot. Twitch. "Wham-o", a vicious strike and I was in business. A very good bass. But disappointingly, not the big fish! I played him in and strung a seventeen incher - my largest of the trip so far.

After a couple of casts, I repeated as before - same cast, same drift. The popper approached the boulder. A slight twitch, the rubber legs trembled slightly. Blast! A terrific strike - surely on enormous smallmouth! But, never to be mine; the four-pound leader, perhaps frayed slightly from the previous battle snapped. Gone was the popper and the bass which I never even saw except for the explosion of the strike - and then only tenuously.

I made my way to the water's edge, sat down on a log to regroup and gather my wits. What a fish! Bigger than my giant of eight years ago? I'll never know. But maybe!

During the late 50's and early 60's we did make quite a few trips of Little River and Glover. My life had changed a lot over the past ten years. I was now teaching, and this was to be my life's profession. Of necessity, fishing the wild river became a secondary interest. Nonetheless we still had a lot of fun. Eurith and our two kids, Jon and Sherri, enjoyed camping. Living on a teacher's salary, we could afford this, though for a while, at least, not much else.

We grew to depend more and more on Little River. It was much closer than the other two rivers, still had good fishing and good swimming places for the youngsters. When on Little River we either camped at the mouth of Cloudy Creek or crossed via the low water bridge, drove about a mile farther east and turned to the north on an old logging road. It was rough but always passable. Our camp area here lay alongside a big hole of the river. It was heavily shaded by hardwoods and pines.

Below this large hole of water lay a series of smaller holes separated by rocky shoals. A feeder creek from the north ran beautiful clear water into the first of these holes. This was a favorite area. Smallies and black perch were very active at the mouth of this creek and, by standing quietly in knee-deep water at the south side of the river I could cast a fly, usually a popper, to the rocks and other cover all the way to the creek mouth. By playing the fish quietly and carefully it was possible to catch several, sometimes as many as a half-dozen, before so much action turned them off. I never kept a single fish from this hole.

We fished the other pot holes on down-river for eating fish. In addition to the sunfish; black perch, long ear and an occasional bluegill, and smallmouth, we frequently caught largemouth and spotted bass. Large mouths were decidedly inferior, as fighters, but the spots were almost the equal of the smallies. If all three species of bass were hitting we generally strung the large-mouths and spots, releasing the smallies - an indication of the esteem we held for them as battlers! They actually were the best eating of the three species. I've always believed that their predominately crawfish diet accounted for this. The spots were almost as good as the smallies.

Uncle Fate was fond of setting a limb line or two in some of their "potholes". We'd tie them to a button bush or willow on the deeper side of the hole and bait the one or two hooks with a small, live perch. Our intended quarry was flat-head catfish, a number of which inhabited each of these holes. We'd usually catch several of these on each trip, though never any larger than about four pounds.

Once, we set a limb-line around a big brush pile stacked by high water near the south bank of the campsite hole. Uncle Fate allowed as to the fact that we'd probably have a big catfish the next morning. Sure enough, when I checked the line at daybreak, the limb it was tied to was bent down to the water and was shaking and jerking spasmodically. Obviously, I had a big fish. Carefully, I grasped the line and pulled it free of the brush, but rather too easily. This was no catfish! When I pulled the fish to the surface, to my amazement, I had a huge largemouth bass. Later, at camp, it weighed six and a half-pounds, the biggest bass I've seen in the wild rivers.

Dad and Uncle Fate wanted to fish a medium sized hole about a mile upstream from this campground. We crossed the river to the north bank and followed a logging road most of the way to the hole. Then a game trail for the rest of it. A person had to "keep his eyes open" while walking these trails because of the possibility of encounters with cottonmouths, copperheads, or rattlers. We seldom actually saw any of these snakes. I believe that a reason of this was the abundance of free-range razorback hogs which would not hesitate to dine on such critters.

When we reached our objective, Dad and Uncle dropped out to fish the lower end of the hole and the shoal below it. They'd fish opposite sides of the river. I stayed on the trail, moving upstream to the upper end and the shoal leading into it. As I neared this upper end I began hearing strange sounds from the river. Splashing, groaning sounds interspersed with grunting, crushing noises and squeals. Curious, I very quietly worked my way to the source of all this disturbance. It obviously was in the shoal.

Two razorback sows, full grown, and about ten or twelve of their offspring, were having a ball! A breakfast party! They would submerge their head, pick up something from the bottom, raise their head and grunting in apparent ecstasy, crunch and swallow what they'd found. Debris from this activity dropped into the water and floated down- stream into the hole, I could see activity near the point where the moving stream entered. Fish apparently liked what the hogs were feeding on too!

I moved closer. Finally, I could see what the sows and their brood were doing. This shoal area, unlike most on the river, was not all rock-bottom but had areas of firm-packed mud. Thousands upon thousands of fresh water clams or "mussels" inhabited this mud. Some were as big as a man's hand. In these low-calcium waters, rimmed with granite, they were relatively thin shelled. The pig family was gorging themselves on the clams and in the process, chumming the end of the hole I'd come to fish!

Quietly and carefully, so as not to disturb and scare the swine from their breakfast, I tied on the McGinty bee with a tiny sliver of fly-rind attached. Moving into casting range I began working the fish feeding on the clam chum. Most of them were black perch - and a lot of them were big ones. The fishing was fantastic. I caught about thirty, stringing around half that number before the fishing tapered off and finally stopped. The pig family moved off to other things, bellies full after a huge breakfast of clams on the half-shell! Dad and Fate had a little trouble with my story, but the evidence was on my stringer!

Uncle Rob had always said that when camping we would leave the woods as we found them. If we could bring civilizations amenities in, then we could haul out the resulting trash. He was adamant about this and so our trips home always included our camp garbage and trash. I never saw even one tiny piece of paper or a tin can, or a bottle left behind. We all developed the habit of checking our campsite just before we left. Years after his death we were still following Uncle Rob's wishes on this.

In 1964 Eurith and I, moved with our kids to the Dallas metroplex. We'd both been offered teaching jobs at a much better salary than I'd had during our four years at Hugo. And as with every young couple, financial security was one of the important factors to be considered in our life. As a result of this move and other changes in our lives, our days on these wild rivers came to an end.

We made a one-day trip to Little River in 1979. Dad and I caught a lot of fish but the trip, to me, was a heartbreaker. The Dierk's timber operation had been sold. The new owner, a huge corporation, was practicing clear cutting and the elimination of hardwoods from the forest. Herbicides were used often for the eradication of these "weed trees". A spokesman of the company was quoted as saying they were not interested in managing for clear, clean streams or wildlife production. I believed them after seeing what they'd done to our primitive camping areas and the rivers.

PART 2: THE CREEK

 **24 THE CREEK AND THE WETLANDS**

In 1942, my dad was hired as principal for the high school at Yuba. We moved to our new place in November and for the next half-century, it was home.

Even though I was only seven years old at the time, I'd already started developing interests that have persisted for the rest of my life. The outdoors, the woods, creeks and lakes became my school, my refuge, my home—my main interest in life other than my family.

Our house was an old one. The owner of the place, C.C. Hatchett, a Durant lawyer, told my dad that it was at least 30 years old at that time. We had a good garden spot, a large cedar-log barn, and best of all, from my viewpoint, a beautiful creek just a few yards from the back door.

The creek was clean, clear and unpolluted. I quickly learned that it held a huge variety of fascinating aquatic life—many kinds of fish, bullfrogs, crawfish, water snakes, fresh-water clams and hosted a variety of birds and other wildlife. It had its beginnings in a patch of woods approximately a half-mile north of highway 78. It crossed the highway, beneath a bridge, a few hundred yards west of the Yuba General Store.

The creek bed was fairly deep since it lay in rather soft sandy soil that was easily eroded. It was mostly a flat-bottomed stream and had no large bulky rocks. There were, however, many exposed beds of small to mid-sized gravel. I loved these gravel beds. The rocks were of many colors and kinds, and to my delight, a good place to look for arrowheads. During a normal, flood-free summer the creek was clear with shoals and running water interspersed with flat, straight areas. There were a number of bends, and therefore, holes of water which were deeper—up to 5 or 6 feet. Such holes were excellent for swimming and diving and, usually held a good population of big fish and an occasional bass or crappie.   Around some of the bends and also at the mouths of tributary branches, banks had caved in. These areas supported a nice growth of wild-onions which I quickly learned to utilize.

The pasture which accompanied the house, about 160 acres of it, was a mix of open meadows and forest. The forest or woods predominated. It had a huge variety of trees, vines, and shrubs. I quickly learned the location of the 2 or 3 kinds of plum bushes, grapevines, rotting logs and their mushrooms, and decaying brush piles with their complement of poke-sallet plants. You see, not only was I interested in the wild critters—rabbits, squirrels, fish, frogs, and birds, (yes, even snakes!), but edible wild plants gained my interest. I was perfectly willing to pick a meal of woodland veggies, cook 'em, and eat 'em with a couple of roasted field lark breasts and fried fish! Mother wasn't too keen about some of this, particularly the wild mushrooms that were so good when fried in real butter. My dad showed me the ones that he knew were safe and, finally, was able to obtain a pamphlet from the Oklahoma Wildlife Department dealing with edible wild mushrooms of southeastern Oklahoma. I used the pamphlet a lot, finally losing it, but by that time I'd learned about the "good ones." At least I never got sick from eating them and have always enjoyed them. Mother would often tell me to go pick a mess of poke greens and wild onions for supper, and these, along with fish from the creek, cornbread and a bowl of pinto beans, made for a delicious meal.

I learned about and consumed the nuts from bull nettles also. I learned how to separate the nuts from the terrible, spiny capsule enclosing them—got a few jabs though before I got it right! Honey locust pods have sweet edible pulp—don't' eat the seeds from those pods though! And learn to distinguish honey locust from black locust. Leave black locust alone. Deadly! Cockle-burr pods have a nice kernel in their center. Burr oak acorns—largest of our native acorns—can be peeled and eaten raw. They are a lot like sweet potato slices. Other acorns can be consumed but must be first leached with hot water to remove tannic acid, and then they can be roasted and crushed into flour, then cooked into pancakes. Lamb's quarters, common around garden and barnyard fences, can be cooked in a mix with poke greens or by themselves. But be sure to thoroughly wash 'em.

Blackberries, strawberries, red haws (hawthorns), black haws (like prunes), plums, choke-cherries, may-pops, and cactus tunas can all be eaten raw or made into jams and jellies. In this part of America, the south-central and south-east, there are numerous species of wild grapes. They're not great raw because of their acidity, but they make the world's best jelly! Common wild grapes in this area include summer grapes, possum grapes, mustangs, and muscadines. These last two <u>are not</u> the same species and, for best results, must be treated differently when utilized. Just don't confuse these edible ones with false grapes (amleopsis which are in the same family, and although they are not really toxic, they have such a bad flavor that even the wild critters won't touch 'em.

Commonly occurring plants which may be used as edible greens, but are usually not, include common chickweed (yes, the lawn pest!), dandelions, curly dock, sheep sorrel and many others too numerous to discuss here. Tubers such as those from nut grass and hog peanuts are highly edible. They must be thoroughly washed, the brown coat peeled away, and then boiled until tender. Nut grass, the commonly despised invader of gardens and lawns, may be eaten raw after washing and peeling.

Teas can be made from sumac berries (delicious), golden-rod blooms and leaves, blackberry and dewberry leaves, dried persimmon leaves, mulberries, rose hips, sage, and sassafras (both leaves and bark).

Wild mustards and peppergrass commonly are used as spices as are chile pequins, a member of the pepper family.

There are many, many other wild plants which have been widely utilized by past generations, but are largely ignored at the present time. I've included in this discussion those which I have tried most often. Anyone gathering wild foods should acquaint themselves with identification, precautions and methods of utilization. I've consumed all of these and found that, properly prepared, they are delicious!

A few yards west of our barn the largest tributary of our creek entered. Though smaller than the main creek it carried a very large volume of water during the rainy season and maintained fairly deep holes during most summers. Adjacent to this branch were a number of room-sized "flat holes" in the woods that filled with overflow water. These holes, often a foot or so deep usually contained a variety of minnows and small sunfish. Continuing westward, the branch crossed an old abandoned road which had led from highway 78 to a couple of homes near the west end of the Hatchett property. A culvert in the old road allowed freedom of movement for water during the wet season. The creek ran for a hundred yards or so through a ditch alongside the roadbed then turned west for a short distance before terminating in a large pothole which was the receptacle for grassland drainage from the south. All of this territory was good fishing in season.

In an easterly direction from our house, the creek crossed highway 78 again. This bridge was much larger and capable of handling a huge volume of water during the spring floods. A necessity because, at times, the creek volume swelled to such proportions that the water level extended from the 78 embankment all the way across to our back yard fence! Then the creek was a wild, untamed miniature river. During calmer seasons though, it was a clear beautiful stream with many twists and turns and, therefore, a lot of holes just right for swimming and fishing.

Another tributary entered from the south about 50 yards from the east bridge. This branch drained a lot of pastureland and Mr. Younger's farmland. Though it had a deep bed it held permanent water in only a few spots. There were only a few bushes along its length and no deep holes. In order to reach SH78 in our car, we had to cross a wooden bridge which could be a ticklish thing during the flood season. I learned to fly-fish in this creek. As stated earlier, it held a lot of sunfish—mostly green sunfish (goggle-eyes) and long-ears which were smaller but voracious bug-eaters and were great fly-rod fish.

Past SH 78 the creek was almost hidden by dense willow growth. There were a number of deep, though narrow, holes which usually held a good number of big sunfish. Just before reaching the cultivated bottomland east of Yuba, the creek made a right turn and headed straight south to join Brown's Creek and thus, flow to the river. In this north-south area, the creek was heavily levied so as to prevent flooding of cotton and corn patches. Brown's Creek was probably a dozen or so miles long. Not as a crow flies, but counting its many curves and meanders. In eons past, it had been a tributary of the river, but for many years, has run through the old bed of the river, with the main body of Old Red now a couple of miles to the south and east.

In fairly recent times there had been cut-off lakes extending for several miles along the old river bed, but these old lakes have virtually disappeared now thanks to erosion and bulldozers. A sharp-eyed observer can easily make out their pathways and beds. They were good fishing holes and were even better for waterfowl and fur-bearing animals such as rackety-coons, possoms, mink, and in historic times, bear, cougar and deer.

Many of the people who lived in this area years ago depended upon these resources for subsistence. Eurith's Uncle Henry Hines spent most of his boyhood in the Brown's Creek bottom. There were a number of families who farmed the open, cleared land bordering this heavily-wooded wilderness, but Henry's family lived deeper in the woods than the rest. He and I were talking about this one day and he told me about the fishing and hunting he'd enjoyed as a boy. He'd once killed a 5 ½ foot rattlesnake just

64

off the front porch., He also said the battles for survival against the critters—wolves, coyotes, and bobcats—were a constant thing. These animals were often after chickens, guineas, calves, and any other livestock they had. Nevertheless, they lived a number of years in that home. I actually saw this "home in the woods" while on a bird hunting foray with my dad and stepbrother, Winfred, in the 1960s. Surprisingly, the house looked to be in a still-livable state. It's gone now—dozers. This whole area, the flood plain, former river bed, and swamp was a wet-land supreme at one time. Land use and abuse have pretty much obliterated it now.

Southwest of our house, about half a mile, was a wetland. It lay in the heart of a heavily wooded area covering about 160-200 acres. The lake, if you could call it that, had a maximum surface area of probably 20-30 acres. During rainy months it filled to capacity and held water to a depth of about four to five feet max. Water drained from it to Brown's Creek about an eighth of a mile south. There was no drainage ditch or channel, at least not in the years that I knew it. Instead the drainage was gradual across a broad, grassy flat area slightly lower than the lake shore. In spite of the slow-drainage rate, the lake generally would empty itself during dry summers, and the only water remaining was in two ponds so ancient that the tupelo gum trees, immediately at the water's edge, had grown their roots out into the ponds. Sometime in the long ago past, these ponds were dug by a team, probably mules, pulling a wedge blade. The dams, or levees, were washed down and quite low, and the ponds were only about a couple of feet deeper than the rest of the lake bottom. Even so, they held water during the hottest summer most years, and so were utilized by a big variety of critters as a drinking source.

Because the drainage from the lake entered Brown's Creek and was so gradual, the lake was restocked every time it overflowed. The result was a variety of fish ranging from creek shiners to long-nose gar 3 ½ feet to 4 feet long. During the winter months of a wet year, shiners, shad and other bait fish were enormously abundant. At that time, the water would be almost crystal clear and various aquatic plants would spring up throughout the lake and along the shoreline. It would become a waterfowl paradise, and I've seen it, literally, covered with mallards and many other species of duck. Of course, such a place gets its share of rough-necks like water snakes, snapping turtles, and a couple of ten or eleven year old guys like my buddy, Gerald, and me. This wetland was generally ignored by most of the residents of the Yuba community. There were no posted signs, no piles of cans or of other trash—just a clean, clear, and relatively pure, wet wilderness.

One year a family moved into a log house situated on the southwest side of the woods and about a few hundred yards from the lake. The house had been there a long time and was pretty dilapidated, as were the out buildings. The family included a couple of kids—stepbrother and sister—who were classmates of mine in school, Donald Ray Baker and Virginia Gibson. They moved away after a short year or so. They were nice, and I hated to see them go.

Years ago, when I was a grown man and hunting squirrels and other small game, I visited these and other old ruins extending along an old road in a westerly direction from these woods. The homesteads were abandoned with some houses still standing, but empty for years. Farm implements were still sitting where they had been parked—though now they were rusted and useless. I wondered about the people who had lived there. It was almost as though I could feel their spirits still there. Needless to say, these were strange, sad sights and times.

Gerald Swindle and I were kindred spirits. We loved to fish and, even more, to roam the woods. He had two dogs. One was a bulldog type — big, maybe a forerunner to today's pit bulls. The other was equally big and was a German police-type dog. They loved to go with us and strangely enough, Gerald had complete control of them. Only a word or two from him brought instant obedience—a remarkable thing

Gerald lived with his mother, brother, Kip, and the two dogs in a little shotgun house at the east side of Lonnie Osborne's tract of land. Life was hard for them, and to this day, I still don't know how they survived. He and I spent lots of time around the wood with the two dogs. We fished al lot in the creeks and in the old lake, and at times, hunted squirrels and rabbits with an old single-shot 22 rifle. He was a crack shot with this. Me—not so good at this time!

One day, when the lake was full in a rainy summer, Gerald, the dogs, and I explored around to the south end of the woods. We spotted a big water snake enjoying the sun while lying on a big log in about eight or ten inches of water. Deciding to have some fun with the snake, we sicced the dogs on it. They took the command joyously and fully! However, the snake wasn't alone! In no time at all, the dogs and, only God knows how many, snakes were in a melee of epic proportions! It seemed that snakes were everywhere with the dogs were mouthing them and slinging them away. We were almost in a state of eye-popping, open-mouthed fear and panic. <u>Finally</u> it ended with snakes swimming back to their refuges and the dogs with a self-satisfied look of smugness on their faces! Gerald and I each swore we'd been bitten numerous times, but when calmer, close inspections were done there was no indication of such a thing. We decided then that one experience of that kind was more than enough! However, the dogs and us did have other adventures.

One day we hunted a creek north of SH 78. The dogs were sniffing and poking into brush-piles along the creek bank when suddenly they found something they really liked. This time though it was almost more than they could handle. A dark, furry form shot out from the brush-pile, grabbed the bulldog's lower lip in its teeth, bit through the lip, then released it leaving a howling, bleeding canine while it and scampered along the creek to another brush-pile. "What is that thing?" we asked of each other. It moved so fast we couldn't tell! The dogs finally drove it from the second brush-pile, attacked it paying dearly for their brashness, and, eventually, chased it up a willow tree. Now, we could see it clearly. "It's a mink!" said my partner. "We need to kill it because its hide is worth a lot of money," he said. "How do we get it out of the tree," I said. So we sat down and talked about it. Luckily, I guess, I'd brought my Red Ryder BB gun. I told Gerald that maybe if I shot the critter it would come down the tree. "Yeah, and probably get us," said Gerald. We finally, though reluctantly, worked out a plan. He found a sturdy piece of tree limb. I planned on shooting BBs at the mink, and if it jumped at me from the tree, Gerald was going to beat it off with the stick. Well, I must have shot that poor mink a dozen times before he finally leaped from the tree. The dogs were on him in an instant and, finally, were able to end its life. Gerald picked it up, and we looked at it. Bedraggled, torn by the teeth of the dogs and full of BBs from my not-so-expert shooting it looked as though it wasn't even worth a quarter, much less the "lots of money" that Gerald had claimed.

We sat down on a log and rested a while. Gerald said, "I know what we'll do. I'll give it to Rayburn Smith to skin. He's always trapping coons and possums and taking their hides to Durant,. I'll tell him that if he'll take this mink and skin and sell it to Pruitt Produce, we'll give him half of the money." We looked askance at each other—something just didn't sound right about this plan. But, "OK," I said. We didn't know what else to do.

Later, when I told my dad about this, he tried to keep from laughing. I heard him and Mom talking about it after supper. For some reason, they were doing a lot of laughing and giggling. "We'll not say anything to him about it," I heard Dad say, "Experience is the best!"

A few days later I was at Gerald's house, and he told me how the deal with Rayburn worked out. "Rayburn said that the produce guy laughed at the condition of the hide. It was so beat up that he wouldn't give him a thing for it. So Rayburn just threw it away." I thought about this a while and said to Gerald, "Do you think he is telling the truth?" "I don't know," Gerald replied. "Some people think he lies a lot." We talked about it a little more, and I finally said in my tough guy voice, "We oughta whip his ass!" Gerald looked at me. "Rayburn is 19 or 20 years old and weighs 200 pounds at least, and you want me and you to whip his ass? We're 10 years old and weigh maybe 75 pounds. I think you are crazy! Just forget it!" "Well," I said, "we could sic the dogs on him." Gerald just looked at me and shook his head. That was the end of the mink episode.

We went on with our swimming, fishing, and hunting for a while. Then one day I went up to Gerald's house. No one was there, it was empty and vacant. A few days later my dad had heard that they had moved to Arizona or New Mexico. I never heard from Gerald again, but I still think of him often.

I've often wondered about the origin of the little lake and the forest. In walking about the countryside as I did when I was young, it became apparent to me that Red River, sometime in the distant past, in its meandering way, almost certainly ran its waters several miles north of its present bearing. Old river beds and banks eroded by wind and water and grown up in forests, then decimated by man's activities, seem to the careless observer to be of little consequence. But, if one looks carefully and studies the countryside thoroughly, he can see that the river, its sloughs, backwaters, and cut-offs did exist and did support a myriad of aquatic and forest life and furnished a livelihood for the people who lived there.

PART 3: LAKE TEXOMA

25 THE BIG LAKE

In 1952 Earl left the river bottom taking his family to the prairie which was a few miles west of Yuba. He and Uncle Henry frequently joined Uncle Clarence in fishing Lake Texoma. Clarence and Aunt Ellen, by this time, were fishing commercially for catfish with trotlines. When time from farming allowed, Earl and Jewell, Henry and Pearl, joined Clarence and Ellen at their camp near Widow Moore Point just below the mouth of the Cumberland Cut.

At this time the upper end of Texoma was deep, open water. The lake was a broad expanse with little siltation evident. There were depths of 35 to 40 feet almost all the way to the Cut. Fishing was tremendous during these years. Earl and his brothers became experts at trot lining. Three or four days at the Widow Moore campsite frequently yielded over a hundred pounds of dressed catfish. They had a ready market for disposing of their catch. A number of their customers lived in the Yuba community and across the river in Texas. When Earl and Jewell returned from the lake, a few phone calls were made, and quickly the fish were sold. They cared for their catfish extremely well—never losing any because of spoilage. People knew this and their catfish were always in demand. If a huge catch, in poundage, was made early in their trip, they frequently took a load into Durant. Buyers from Durant, including some restaurant owners would converge on market square and the fish quickly would be sold. Earl, Clarence, and Henry were able to keep their catch alive and healthy by using live boxes in several feet of water. Usually on the last day of such a trip, the fish would be dressed and place on ice. They were never filleted, just skinned, gutted and the heads removed.

Earl's fishing rig evolved into a compact efficient system which served for many years. His pick-up was replaced with an old blue school bus which was converted into a wonderful camper. His boat was a fourteen or sixteen foot deep-V Lone Star propelled by an 18 hp to 25 hp motor—usually a Johnson or Evinrude. When on such trips for catfish, practically all the waking hours involved running lines, catching bait, moving lines and cleaning fish. It was a busy time! They ate well on these trips, cooking over a campfire or the gas cook-stove in the bus. Often, Earl's brothers and nephews joined them and this made for some rousing games of dominos!

26 A DESPERATE TIME

On a spring day in 1952, Earl and Jewell drove to Widow Moore Point. Clarence and Ellen had camped there for several weeks and the catfishing had, to put it mildly, been sensational. When they arrived they found Aunt Ellen in tears. Winds had blown from the southwest for several days, as is common in the springtime, and Clarence had been unable to run his lines which he had set near the west bank. The high winds combined with the distance across that arm of the lake made the boat journey to his lines extremely hazardous. By then, they had exhausted their food supply, needed medicines, had no money, and were depending on their fishing proceeds to bring in enough money for their needs. Their situation was desperate.

Clarence decided to try to make the trip over to the lines but was not going to let Ellen go with him—she couldn't swim and the lake was dangerous. His boat for this trip was a 14 foot Lone Star. It was a safe, seaworthy craft. His motor was the problem. His 18 horsepower Johnson had quit running, and he was left with the spare he always took along—a 10 horsepower Mercury. It was a good, reliable motor, but was it powerful enough to do the job in such a windy sea? Waves and wind were tremendous but Clarence felt that he had to attempt the trip.

By moving slowly and carefully, Clarence maneuvered the boat until he was lost from sight. The distance to his lines was about 1 ½ miles—a long trip which normally should not be undertaken in such weather conditions. But, their situation was desperate! And so Aunt Ellen tearfully told this to Earl and Jewell. She was understandably in fear for his life!

Earl and Jewell comforted her as best they could. Earl suggested they put on a pot of coffee and begin preparation for breakfast. Maybe if she stayed busy Ellen could relax a bit. But Ellen was upset because she and Clarence had no food or coffee. Their plight had gotten so bad. Earl assured her that he and Jewell had plenty of rations and so the women turned to making breakfast.

Earl walked to the open point so he could have a good view of the lake in the direction of Clarence's journey. For a while he was silent. Then after about half an hour, "I see a speck across the lake," he said. "It's moving this way." The "speck" slowly but surely grew and became Clarence's boat. Earl said, "Something's wrong. It's so low in the water. It must have swamped." Clarence navigated through seas expertly, gunning when necessary, and all the while keeping the prow into the waves. A broadside blow would have been a disaster! The boat was almost foundering. Earl said he thought it was about to sink, it'd taken on so much water. Finally, after almost an hour, Clarence pulled into the little sheltered bay just below their campsite. Earl and the two women rushed to meet him.

"Look at this boat," Earl exclaimed. Amazingly, there was little water in it. It was filled half-way to the gunnels with big catfish! Clarence's trotlines had been loaded. The high winds had triggered a catfish feeding frenzy! There were several hundred pounds of squirming fish in the boat.

Earl and Clarence carried the fish to Earl's pick-up. Some of the cats were so large that both men had to carry a single fish! They emptied Earl's camper of groceries, bedding and other camping equipment, then placed the catfish inside. They had a dozen big burlap (tow) sacks for this purpose: thoroughly wetted, they'd cover the fish and keep them alive and frisky until they arrived at Durant's market square.

About three hours later they returned to camp—the pick-up was loaded with groceries and fishing supplies. Clarence still had a couple of hundred dollars in his pocket after buying their supplies. The biggest fish had weighed seventy-eight pounds. Another fish had been a sixty-one pounder, and the rest were from just under twenty to forty-eight pounds.

Earl said that this was the biggest catch he'd ever seen—total number of big fish. Only Clarence's skill at trotlining and his boatmanship had made it possible!

 **27 FISHING THE CUT**

When Texoma was built, the Cumberland Cut was dug in order to divert the Washita River away from the oilfield in a small part of the river bottom. A dike was constructed across the river and extended parallel to the Cut all the way to the Little City and Cumberland highway. The Washita, as a result, ran straight east for several miles before joining the rest of the lake. The mouth of the Cut or Washita occurred at the confluence of a large creek from the north. This was Kansas Creek.

This area became a famous fishing spot. If the main lake was low during the spring, migrating fish, including buffalo and catfish, could reach the mouth of the Cut, but no farther. Their upstream progress was interrupted by a falls—relatively broad and deep. The pool at the base of the falls became absolutely loaded with fish attempting to move upstream to spawn. Though the big fish were cat and buffalo, they were totally overshadowed by the millions of sand bass attempting to go upriver.

People from hundreds of miles around came to the Cumberland Falls during the sandie spawn. A bait shop and boat ramp were constructed and business was booming!

At first the fisherman used brightly colored spoons. They were enormously effective. Then someone tried a snag rig with a heavy weight and stout treble hook—this worked even better!

During the peak times, catches frequently numbered in the hundreds for a family adept at snagging. In addition to the sandies, enormous carp, buffalo, and blue catfish were caught. Even black bass and crappie became caught up in all the excitement and paid dearly for it as they, too, became snag victims. The banks would become littered with less desirable fish such as gar, drum, carp and buffalo. Snaggers were going home with huge strings of sandies, cats, black bass and crappie. The Wildlife Department, concerned that such carnage could seriously lessen the Texoma fishery sent rangers to patrol the area. Gamefish—including channel and blue cats, paddle fish, bass, and crappie—were declared off limits for snagging. Many citations were written as fishermen failed to follow the rules. All of us fishing at that time visited the Falls and snagged at least a few—some of us paid fines for the joy of the experience!

When the spawning run was over, the Washita, around the Falls, became enormously popular for rod and reel conventional catfishing. Huge blue cats could be taken from the bank using surf rods and cut shad for bait. In 1956, the publication of the Wildlife Department's "Oklahoma Game and Fish" ran an article dealing with catching big blues at the mouth of the Cut. This article featured a full page photograph in addition to a couple of pages of text. The photograph showed the proprietor of the bait shop, Oren Robertson, and his partner in the shop, landing a huge cat of over 40 lbs. Many years later, Mr. Robertson became friends of Earl and Henry—he fished the Widow Moore area with trotlines, too.

Nowadays, in 2012, the Falls at the mouth of the Cut are gone— buried under many feet of silt. The foundations of the bait shop and the old boat ramp are still visible if a person looks hard enough. Silt has claimed the whole area, and the space that was once a large part of Lake Texoma is now a willow forest. The mouth of the Washita extends far into the main area of the lake and pours its muddy waters into the lake at a point southeast of the Cumberland Community. This point of the lake is, at this time, virtually abandoned. Access to Widow Moore is now non-existent and completely cut off from the main lake, as is the old camping area at Widow Moore Point and the huge expanse of open, deep water where Clarence, Earl, and Henry set their lines—all a part of the past and existing only in the memories of those of us, lucky enough to know and love those times.

But, before all the siltation took its toll, Earl and the boys— Clarence, Henry, Lee, Richard, and often, Jess Branch and Henry Staton— fished the Cut. It was a catfish and sand bass paradise! They often camped in the area around the bridge just southwest of Fort Washita In these days, the 50s, 60s and early 70s, the Cut was open with good camping areas where picnic tables were setup, and there were many bays, coves, and points in addition to the main river. Fishing was exceptional to put it mildly. Trotlines would often yield hundreds of pounds of cats for a night's work. Sandies and crappie were abundant.

Lake Texoma, in its early years, extended all the way to the mouth of Pennington Creek at Tishomingo. A resort area, Butcher Pen, became famous for its springtime crappie fishing. Sandies were there by the jillions,

Dad and I made a camping trip with Earl and the guys in 1953 just before I started college. I enjoyed going with the catfishermen to run the lines. One night, besides catfish, a huge number of big sandies were on the

75

lines. One of these was a 4 ½ pounder! I've never seen another sandie that large.

28 THE FLOOD

A terrible drought encompassed the area in 1956. Ponds dried up, creeks, became just ribbons of dry dust and gravel. The level of Lake Texoma dropped to 591 feet above sea level. This was twenty-six feet below normal elevation. Vast areas of lake-bottom were exposed. The surface area of the lake, normally over 90,000 acres, dropped to less than half that; This drought had persisted for several years, but reached a desperation point in '56. Much of the lake-bottom had grown up in willows and weeds.

But this all changed in 1957. Rains began in January and persisted through the spring finally tapering off that summer. The lake had a rise of over 50 feet! It came around the spillway for the first time ever. On the rare occasions when this happens, there is no control over the Red River downstream of the dam. In the spring of '57, this enormous flood filled the Cut almost to the top of the dike. Earl, his brothers, Henry Staton and Jess Branch, and my dad decided to go catfishing. They camped on the dike, near its top. The river was pouring through the Cut so swiftly that their fishing was confined to the back waters. This was a pretty extensive area and heavily forested. Trotlines were strung from one tree top to another and baited with cut shad. Apparently these overflow waters were swarming with cats—the first night of fishing yielded over 200 pounds of dressed fish. The second night was just as good. Some of these fish were in the 20 to 30 pound range. For several weeks the guys fished the dike area. My dad even bought and assembled a trotline of his own—something he normally didn't care about.

Eventually, the lake level began dropping and the fishing in the Cut dramatically decreased in quality. The guys "folded their tents" and went home. Below the dam, Red River flooded the surrounding land for two months. Fishing in the Red, later that summer, was great!

29 SHYSTERS, SIDEWINDERS AND CHAMPS

Dad, my sister Doris, and I fished the Cumberland Cut on May 20, 1956. Eurith and I were to be married on the 23rd and Dad said I should have one last fishing trip! We packed a picnic lunch and headed for the river. Mom stayed behind as she was busy with the wedding.

We fished a spot with good road access about a half-mile downriver from the primitive camping area near the Cumberland dike. For a good part of the morning we had little action; just a few small sandies here and there. Our style of fishing was simple. Walk the bank and cast, while looking for a school of sandies.

Our tackle was as simple as our technique. Rods were 5 ½ foot whippy fiberglass; reels were inexpensive Shakespeare bait casters and new-fangled Zebco spincasters. Our lures were a mix of Shyster spinners and Sidewinder spoons. We preferred ¼ oz. Shysters with a yellow body and black polka dots and silver blade. Our favorite Sidewinders were ½ oz and gold-colored. We liked both the Shyster and Sidewinder if the attached treble hook had a yellow feather tied to the hook shank.

For a couple of hours action remained slow. Then about mid-morning Dad tied into a big one. The fish was tough and strong; a real fighter. Dad beached him—a huge sandie—over 2 lb. of striped, furious fish. The surface of the river exploded with feeding fish. A school of big sandies had driven a school of shad into the small cove we were fishing! Frantic bait skittered across the surface attempting to escape the lightning fast predators. We clipped the Shysters from our lines and went with the gold Sidewinders., They were easier to cast and not as likely to twist the line.,

For an hour it was virtually a fish on every cast. We tossed the sandies on the beach a we unhooked 'em. My sister gathered 'em in a five gallon bucket filling it! We began releasing fish and taking an occasional rest break. The school finally moved off downriver. We were pooped!

As we dumped the fish into Dad's rusty old steel ice chest for the trip home, we counted 78 big sandies plus four big crappie and a couple of nice largemouth bass that had joined the fray. This was an entirely legal number of sand bass to keep since there were no limits on quantity or size in those days We estimated that we had released another 40 to 50!

The Cumberland Cut, or just "the Cut" as it were known, was a fantastic spring fishery for sandies making their spawning run from the big lake. It was almost a good for catfish, both channel cats and big blues. Trotliners really "cleaned up" on the cats during the spring and early summer.

The Cut, until the late 70s, showed little evidence of siltation. There were many coves and bays off of the main river. These were great areas for crappie and black bass in the spring time. One of the best spots was stump patch just west of the Little City Bridge.

Dad and I would usually lay our 12 foot jon boat in his old pick-up , sometimes put in our 10 hp Mercury and tackle, and head for the Cut. We'd stop at Mr. Knight's bait store in Durant, buy a couple of buckets of river shiners and a few snack groceries and pop. Often, we'd not bother with the motor and just take a couple of paddles.

If the water level in the Cut was as we liked it with some of the stumps having their "heads" above water, we'd tie up, bait our hooks with shiners and have at it! Our usual catch might include 20 to 30 big crappie, plus as many sandies, and a scattering of black bass and channel catfish. We'd use our baitcasters, 20 lb. line and, because of the current, a ¾ oz or 1 oz sinker. If we fished in one of the coves off the main river, we'd got our lighter tackle and frequently tossed jigs for the crappie.

As great as the Cut was for crappie and catfish, its claim for fame was the sandies. As noted, spring fishing could be tremendous. It is hard for me to visualize any better. I've seen my father-in-law, Earl, and Uncle Henry seine bait for trotlining in the summertime. At times, shad were very hard to find, but they'd literally load their seine with young sandies.

The mouth of the Cut opened into Texoma at the spot where a small arm of the lake, Kansas Creek, entered. This was a hot-spot almost any spring, but was hottest when the lake level was lower than the Washita River. When those conditions existed, an extensive rapids or "falls" up to 5 or 6 feet high resulted.

During my spring break time in April 1961, I loaded my tackle and headed for this spot. The Falls were just right—for the fishermen! A hundred or more fishermen lined the bank casting into the turbulent, turbid waters. Some were using spoons, some used jigs, and several had rigged heavy weights and trebles for "snagging"—a technique which had been outlawed, but was still in use. Game wardens often had a field day here, not only because of the illegal snagging, but also as a result of many fishermen exceeding bag limits for catfish and black bass. It seemed that almost every fish in the lake was attempting to swim up the Cut! Not true, of course, for a lake as big as Texoma.

My catch for the day was minimal at the mouth of the Cut. I only stayed for an hour or so—too many people in too small an area. The bank was littered with carcasses of shad and gar—victims of being snagged illegally or with more acceptable spoons like 1 oz Mr. Champs which were the favorite.

I left this area and moved to the camping area just west of the bridge. A cove just down the hill from the concrete tables was my goal. I fished until mid-afternoon, taking a break for my usual fishing lunch of potted meat, crackers, pork and beans, and green onions from Dad's garden.

The sandies that perished at the mouth of the Cut were only a tiny fraction of those that managed to navigate the Falls. This became evident to me as the day progressed. Using 3/8 oz Gay Blades, Mr. Champs and Sidewinders on a 6 ½ foot fiber glass rod and Sabra spincaster with 17 lb line, I reaped a rich harvest of fat, spawn-run sandies! Quite a day with a total of 56 good ones!

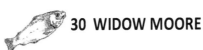 ## 30 WIDOW MOORE

On an April day in 1973, Dad, Winfred and I headed for Widow Moore to hunt for crappie. Heavy spring rains over a period of weeks had elevated the lake level in to the willows and button bushes lining the banks of Starr and Widow Moore Creeks. This was spawning time for crappie and the fish should be congregating in the thick cover. We were pulling my 14 foot Sea King behinds Dad's pickup. My motor was a 9.8 hp Mercury. This was a light, maneuverable outfit well suited for the area we'd fish. We stopped at Mr. Knight's bait shop in Durant for shiners to complement an assortment of jigs which I panned to try.

We launched from the old road-bed at the end of Staff Creek, and motored quietly to a row of partly submerged button bushes in order to begin the day's fishing. We weren't alone. A couple of other boats of fishermen were working some of the abundant cover. "How're ya'll doin?" Winfred called to two elderly fishermen in one of the boats. "Not very well," one gentleman replied. "So far the crappie are scarce and we've only caught a half-dozen or so."

We fished along the Starr Creek channel, testing every brush pile an button bush thoroughly. Our only result was three small crappie of eight or nine inches. Action was slow—to put it mildly.

After an hour or so of this, I told the other two to let me out near a group of button bushes close to shore. I left my bait rod in the boat, taking with me an 8 ft fly rod equipped with a 1/8 oz brown and yellow marabou jig. I'd work this in close to the base of the button bushes as tightly as possible to the cover.

After only a few minutes around the first bush I tried, I felt a light "tick" as a fish hit the jig. The battle was on! The limber fly-rod arced gracefully and the crappie pulled mightily. At least as mightily as he could, considering his size and genetics! The battle was short and the 10 inch fish went on my stringer.

I waded the 75 foot stretch toward the creek channel, keeping the jig as deep into the cover as possible, the fishing wasn't great, in fact, it was quite slow. My two boat-mates had moved into another creek area along the north bank about a couple of hundred yards from me. They were using shiners on light cane poles equipped with 12 lb mono-line, a sinker, hook and floater. I watched them a few minutes. Clearly, their fishing was also pretty slow.

By the time I'd reached the creek channel, I'd strung a total of 5 crappies. They were 9 to 11 inch fish. Good eating size but no big ones. In those days there was no size limit for crappie, and a fat, 7-incher was considered to be an eating-size fish. The creek channel was too deep to wade, and so I turned back to re-fish the button-bush row to the bank. Results were slim, I strung two more fish and released three that were too-small—ones of about 5 or 6 inches.

Dad and Winfred motored up. They'd not had a very productive couple of hours. Between the two they'd kept 7 crappie and one black bass of a couple of pounds. Two of their crappie though, were nice 12 and 13 inches. "Let's go out to the point," Dad said. "We'll see how the catfishermen are doing." The catfishermen he referred to were my in-laws, Earl and Jewell, plus Henry and Pearl, Earl's twin sister.

Widow Moore point marked the area where the big curve or bay opened up into the big lake. A vast body of water extended west and south. The north area was the Cumberland dike and the mouth of the Washita at Kansas Creek. Widow Moore cove had many smaller coves and branches leading into it. These were areas in which crappie and bass fishing could be terrific at times. In the spring, any of the smaller points and the main point itself were excellent for white bass or sandies.

We visited with my in-laws over a cup of fishing coffee for a while. Dad and Winfred were ready to hit the small coves along the south bank for more crappie to add the the ice chest.

Earl told us that some good sandies had been "running" in the area around the point. This was right up my alley! "You go ahead if you want to," I told Dad and Winfred. "I'm going to try for sandies." I retrieved a light 5 ½ ft casting rod and my Ambassadeur reel along with my tackle bag from the boat. They took off for the crappie hunt, and I prepared to fish the area around the point. In my tackle bag was a stringer, long-nosed pliers, a small box of 3/8 oz Gary Blades and a plastic bag of Sidewinders and Mr. Champs. I tied on a ½ oz Sidewinder and waded out just on the east side of the point., A good long cast and I let the spoon hit the bottom in about 12 feet of water. I began a moderate retrieve. The lure traveled only a short distance when, "whack"—a good hit! The sandie was a good one and fought hard. The rod was fairly stiff and the fish tired quickly! I strung the fat 1 ½ pounder.

Subsequent casts produced the same type of result. Most of the sandies were of a size—good, solid 1-1 ½ pounders. A few were larger; approaching a couple of pounds. Good fish and fierce fighters. Occasionally I hang a rock or water-logged log. Sometimes, I'd break off a lure. I stayed with the Sidewinders and Mr. Champs. Their one treble hook simplified removal and enabled be to "get back to it" quicker. I strung about a dozen, then began releasing fish as I caught 'em. And we continued to catch 'em!

After an hour or so, Dad and Winfred returned from their crappie search which had proven to be fishless. From a distance they'd seen Earl and I having a ball with the sandies. "Kelwyn,

You have any extra lures?" Dad asked. I tossed him the sack of Mr., Champs and Sidewinders from my tackle bag, and soon he and Winfred joined the fray. Along about noon, the fishing tapered off. We'd caught a prodigious number of sandies—the chest was full. Dad and Earl filleted a bunch of sandies, Jewell and Pearl peeled onions, fried some potatoes opened a couple of cans of pork & beans while a fresh pot of coffee brewed. We had a real fisherman's lunch! A memorable morning.

31 SPRINGTIME AT THE POINT

Dad and I started early, arriving at Widow Moore point just after day break on April 20, 1974. The morning was cloudy, chilly and misty. This didn't appear to be a good day, weather-wise. We donned our chest waders, tied stringers to our belts and gay-blades to our lines. We each used 5 ½ foot medium bait casting rods I'd built from Fenwick and Lamiglas blanks. My reel of choice was a new 5000C which had been given me my by AP Class. Dad's reel was a battered but efficient Omega-One spin caster. We were using 14 lb. Trilene XT.

"There's a fish striking," Dad said. "Right off the point. Better hurry; they may not be here long."

We stepped into the chill water and whipped our casts to an area where there was some surface activity. Immediately our rods bowed with the weight of heavy fish. The moderately stiff rods took their toll quickly, and we landed thick-bodied sandies of around a pound and a half. We tossed our fish on the gravel bar and hurriedly made our next casts into the same area. Results were identical—except the sandies were even larger than the first pair.

As the morning moved along, the weather deteriorated, the mist increased, and the wind came on--15 to 25 mph, as is common at this time of year. This was not to be a sunny, warm, springtime day but, instead, a damp, blustery, chilly one. But great fishing weather!

After about 20 minutes of non-stop action we took a break for some hot coffee and to string our fish. I'd had a streak of 16 consecutive casts with fish resulting and Dad's results were similar. Our fish were big sandies by any standards. Most were in the one to one and a half pound class, but several were two pounders and we had a few which pulled the De-Liar to two and a half pounds! "We've already caught a big pile of fish, " Dad remarked. "How many of these do we want to clean?" We agreed to release most of the rest.

We each cut back and retied. I decided to try a ½ oz. Hot Spot, but he stayed with the 3/8 oz. Gay Blade. Each lure was in the Smoky Joe pattern—a very realistic shad imitation.

Our lures were equally effective. It became obvious that vast numbers of sandies were feeding off the point and probably would hit any properly presented bait! I tried feather jigs, Little Georges, other patterns of spots and blades, and even small top-water chuggers. Only the chuggers didn't work well. The sandies were obviously tuned in to an underwater shad pattern.

At around 11:15 we took a lunch break—hot coffee from the thermos, pork and beans, rat cheese, and Dad's favorite dish, hot chili-mac from another thermos. Each spring, when fishing season arrived, he'd buy a case of it and by the end of the early crappie and sand-bass season it'd be gone!

We agreed to fish a couple more hours, since the activity had somewhat tapered off, but, with renewed vigor, the bite was still on. The hours went by. Finally Dad said, "It's 3:30. I've had enough." "One more cast," I said. An immediate hit, but this was the smallest of the day. I looked carefully at the fish. Only about 6 inches long, its body was more slender, the pattern of stripes different than the usual sand-bass. There were "parr" marks, similar to those I'd read about on salmon and other saltwater fish.

"Look at this, "I said. "I believe I've caught a baby striper." Dad said to see if I could catch another one. My next cast identical results. Stripers had been stocked in Texoma several years earlier, and I'd read an article, by John Clift, in the Herald, that the biologists had evidence of their spawning. These two tiny stripers and their tribe were to have a profound influence on the rest of my life as a fisherman!

Dad and I cleaned 55 big sandies before leaving the point. We'd released twice that many. My days total was an even 100, and Dad's results were similar. The next Saturday, amazingly, was identical, weather-wise. We brought the family, had a picnic-lunch off the back of the pick-up, and our fishing results were even better! My total was 109 sandies and two small black bass. Dad didn't fish as hard as the week earlier, but the wives and kids

also caught fish. Again, we kept around 40 the rest were released —
springtime fishing at Widow-Moore point, in the old days!

32 FALL FISHING

The fall fishing of 1978 was the first time we began finding
some bigger stripers. During our thanksgiving break, we elected to fish
Widow Moore. The day was cloudy and drizzly with a light southeast
wind. We launched the boat at the big pint. Our plan was to fish till
noon, and then join Eurith, the kids, and Lora for lunch at the point.

The early morning fishing was very slow, and we were
beginning to get very discouraged. But, about 10:30, we saw a bunch of
gulls begin working, big time, near the bluffs at the back end of Star
Creek. We hustled over there as fast as possible. I'd been experimenting
recently with white Sting Ray grubs and had good results. They were
easier to remove from the fish than the Gay Blades and hot Spots we'd
been using. The single big hook made this possible. I'd assembled the
Sting Rays on nice, sharp, 3/8 oz unpainted jig heads and had developed
a pretty good technique for fishing them. It involved casting, letting the
jig sink to the desired depth then retrieving with variable speed and
"twitching" during the retrieve. This imputed a great deal of action to a
lure which had no built in action of its own!

The gulls were frantically hitting the water as we neared them;
I cut down the motor and brought the electric into play. Fish were
blasting into the tightly bunched threadfins. Our first casts with the Sting
Rays were savagely smashed by good fish. We fought them to a
standstill and lifted them into the boat. They were enormously fat
sandies and into the box they went.

The fish stayed in the area for an hour or so, and we continued
to fill our ice chests. Around 11:30, the sandies tapered off, and we took
stock of what we'd caught, retied our lures and prepared to cruise in an
effort to find another school. However, before I could crank up the
outboard, a good fish struck just a few yards away. I made a good cast
into the disturbed water, let the grub drop, and was, immediately, into a
fish much heavier than the sandies we'd been catching.

Dad had also cast into the same area and was locked into another big one. We finally fought the fish down after a couple of drag screeching runs. "Stripers!" Dad said after getting the first look at our adversaries. And so they were. I netted them one at a time since their combined weight might have broken our worn, aging landing net. We'd caught many smaller stripers over the past few years, but nothing over a couple of pounds. These fish were, easily, several times that in weight. I quickly boxed them, and we continued casting.

The fish stayed around this part of the cove for quite a while and were joined by a school of big sandies. We were able to keep up with the fish easily by staying with the birds. It was quite a mix. Our catch included big sandies, more big stripers, and a couple of three pound largemouths, plus four big crappie of one to two pounds. The blacks and crappie seemed to be hanging around the fringes of the action and were just icing on the cake!

I finally tied into a much bigger, fish fought him for a couple of minutes, and then lost him when the relatively light wire hook partially straightened. I figured that he was probably around ten or twelve pounds. Dad even caught and released a big carp of about fifteen pounds, and, illustrating the feeding frenzy we'd just witnessed, I landed a three pound channel cat.

Exhausted from two hours or so of non-stop fighting heavy fish, we motored to the big point for rest and lunch which the ladies had prepared. Our ice chest was full—we'd kept 45 sandies of 1 ½ to 2 lbs, 4 stripers of 6 to 7 lbs each, three big crappie and a nice channel cat. After lunch, we got out our knives and filleting boards and cleaned the fish. We carefully trimmed the red meat from the sides of the stripers having learned by experience that the fillets would be tainted if we left them untouched. We estimated that our catch was probably about 60-70 lbs total live weight. Dad and I had kept several stripers each, released several, and lost a couple of more.

We'd caught our first striped bass in the spring of 1974 while fishing a sand bass blitz of enormous proportions at the big point of Widow Moore. In the ensuing years, we'd caught quite a few fish in the 1 ½-2 pound category. They'd generally been mixed in with schools of sand bass of about the same size. These fish, of around 7 lb that day, were our largest stripers to date, but as it turned out, were only a harbinger of things to come.

Our tackle included Fenwick 5 ½ foot casting rods in #4 and #5 power, plus, for me, an Ambassadeur 5000 loaded with 15 lb line. Dad preferred a spin cast, Zebco Omega One. This was good, sturdy tackle, and it served us well for years.

A week later, December 2nd, I returned to Widow Moore point. The day was a typical fall day; dreary, chilly, cloudy with a breeze from the south. The lake level was low, 611 feet, and the water temperature was 54 . I'd left the boat at home and instead had brought my chest waders. I planned to fish all day, since I was by myself.

Again, I tied on the white Sting Ray grub, was using the 5000C and 555 Fenwick, and my line was 17 lb Stren. I fished Widow Moore point till 1:30 then moved to the 2nd point east. The sandies, big ones, were everywhere! These were heavy fish, many were 2 ½ pounders, and some were crowding 3 pounds. By mid-afternoon I'd caught 45 big sandies, eight black bass averaging two pounds each and five stripers of 2-2 ½ pounds, but no big ones. This was a typical late fall day at Widow Moore—dark, gloomy and windy! I loved it!

33 OCTOBER 1979

Earl and Jewell were camped at Widow Moore point the first week in October. They'd had good luck trotlining and had also caught a bunch of big sandies and a couple of nice stripers. Richard, Eurith's cousin, was camped with them and had come home to bring a batch of dressed catfish for the freezer. He stopped at the house to show us his fish and said that we ought to go on up since our style (lure) of fishing seemed to be good.

So I loaded our tackle, the 14 foot Sea King, and the 15 hp Johnson into the pick-up, and we took off. We arrived at the point about 8:00 a.m., launched the boat and took off. By noon we'd tried all the creeks and points along the Widow Moore shoreline and had nothing to show for our efforts. Our nephew, Eddie, joined me after lunch, and we headed toward a big creek mouth south of the point.

As we neared the creek, we saw bait skipping and swirls of bigger fish. We cast Smokey Joe Gay Blades (3/8 oz) into the melee and immediately had savage strikes and hook-ups. These were terrifically strong, big, voracious sandies. One literally jerked my rod from my hand, and I barely saved it from going overboard.

The school stayed around in a feeding mode for about 2 hours, and Eddie and I boated about 30 big sandies, 2 to 2 ½ pounders, in that time. We also caught about 20 smaller sandies and small stripers after the big ones left.

The next 3 week-ends were very blustery—wind consistently in a range of 20-30 mph. Any boat fishing was out. So, as I frequently have done all my fishing life, I elected for wading!

October 20 was an excellent, a solid day for me with a mix of big sandies, small stripers, an occasional large-mouth, and even a 3 lb channel cat. Dad had similar results, but topped mine with a 6 lb striper. The 3/8 oz Gay-Blades in Smokey Joe, shad, and yellow-green stripes were hot baits.

The pay-off though, came on the following Saturday. Dad had a prior commitment and Eurith didn't want to fight the 30 mph southwesterner, and so, I went to the point by myself. My score for the day was 89 big sandies to 2 ½ lb, 2 large-mouths of a couple of pounds each, 13 stripers to 2 lb, and a couple of eating size channel cats—all on the afore-mentioned Gay Blades. This lure was my main go-to bait for many years. In size and shape, it was a dead ringer for the threadfin shad the predators were gorging on, and fishing didn't get much better!

34 DECEMBER 23, 1980

We were at the Yuba place for Christmas break when Dad and I talked it over and decided to try Widow Moore again. We'd made a half-dozen trips to this great area during October and November, but had not fished it in a month due to winter-like weather. The last trip we'd made, during Thanksgiving break gave only moderately fair results—just a few small stripers, blacks, and sandies, plus one decent striper of 4 ½ lb. We'd used Gay-Blades, Hot Spots, Sting-Ray grubs and pearl wiggle-tail grubs on ¼ and 3/8 oz lead heads.

This day, we started early at the "crappie bluffs" on the north shore. These were so named because a lot of brush had been sunk in 4 to 8 feet of water just off the shore. As a result this usually was a reliable spot for crappie. The deep water just off the bank gradually tailed out to a shallow, stump-filled flat which bordered a fairly deep creek entering the lake about a hundred yards east of the crappie bluff. Often, as we fished this area I'd walk and wade this flat while Dad, using minnows, would fish the brush. As often as not, my forays into the stump-filled flat would yield several keeper size black bass of 2 or 3 pounds plus a smattering of decent sandies.

The deep water of the creek, especially at the mouth, quite often held schools of bait and frequently big sandies and a few stripers. At normal lake levels this area was a terrific winter-time spot—plenty of deep water and acres of flats. Sting Ray grubs—white—on a ¼ oz jig-head, were a favorite winter time lure for me. Accurate casting, to avoid stump snags, was necessary and you had to find the right twitch and cadence in working the jig. I'd had some terrific fishing the year before for huge sandies, good black bass and 4 to 6 pound stripers. So we were quite enthusiastic about our prospects this day.

After a couple of hours, we'd lost some of this enthusiasm, however. Strangely, the fish weren't hitting even though there were gulls and loons working all about the Widow Moore arm. "Let's go try the point," Dad suggested. "Suits me," I said. And we gathered up our tackle, walked to the pick-up and headed for the point at the west edge of the area. This was a favorite spot and required the use of waders. We fished it thoroughly for a couple of hours and had not a touch! Hard to believe...

We had our Chili-Mac, pork and beans, hot coffee lunch and discussed the situation. There were hundreds of big gulls in the cove that were constantly hitting the water and obviously catching plenty of shad. "Maybe there's too much bait," I said. Dad concurred and we discussed going home to pond fish or driving around the east end of the cove in order to access the big hog-back ridge in its center. He suggested that since we were already here at the lake, we might try the hog-back, at least for a while.

So we drove around the end of the cove and parked on the north-side of the ridge in an area which had a lot of brush and logs within a short distance of the bank. While Dad tried this area, I took my casting outfit and lure bag and told him, "I'm going to fish my way out to the point." I tried 3/8 oz Blades, Sting Rays, and a small Pencil Popper. Nothing! As I reached the open-water end of the ridge a group of gulls, squawking as gulls on the attack do, began working just off the end of the point. I tried a Smoky Joe

Gay Blade first. This bait is solid metal, has a lead wiggle plate at the head, and at this size, and color is a dead-on ringer for a thread-fin shad. Down through the years I've probably caught thousands of fish from Texoma on this lure. Unfortunately, it worked NOT AT ALL this day. So I clipped on a four-inch pearl grub with a ¼ oz jig-head and tossed it under a mass of screaming, cartwheeling gulls. I had little hope at this point. But I allowed the lure to free-fall, keeping just a light tension on the line. After a few seconds of dropping, I suddenly felt a very slight "tick" as if a soft-mouthed crappie had mouthed the lure. Reflexively, I set the hook and suddenly the battle was on! The fish, obviously a big striper, made a good long run— indeed powerful—then, it settled down into a battle give and take. My outfit was relatively light for fish like this—the rod was 5 ½ feet long, medium power—standard tackle for Texoma in these days. The reel was a 4500C Ambassadeur loaded with 12 lb Big Game line. Considering the size that the striper appeared to be, I first thought that I was in for a 10 to 20 minute battle. Not to be! In less than 5 minutes the fat striped bass lay exhausted at my feet. Grasping its lower jaw, I walked around the corner of the ridge point and hollered at my dad who was fishing around some logs. He looked up and waved, then walked up the bank and drove the pick-up toward me. I clambered up the bank with my fish and tackle. We examined, weighed, and measured this striper which was longer than we had ever seen, measuring 36 ½ inches and weighing just a couple of ounces less than 23 pounds on the De-Liar. The fish was hog-fat and because its belly was so full, probably was too sluggish to put up a long fight. To this year, 2011, this was my largest striper from the lake.

The rods that Dad and I were using during these early years of striper fishing were short, 5 ½ feet, had short detachable handles, but were, in spite of their smallness, tough and durable. I'd built them myself, from the best quality graphite blanks—his from a Lamiglas blank, mine from a Fenwick. We loved these rods as they were light and, when paired with a good reel, could easily handle a good, big striper or catfish.

For several more years the Widow Moore arm of the lake was a terrific fishing area. It was excellent in all seasons—summer, winter, and in-between. I spent many Saturdays in the fall and winter fishing the north point and then, at times, the coves and points back toward the east end. If the weather was calm, we used my boat. If too windy, then we walked and waded. Often, I'd go there very early on a Saturday then my wife and kids would come later. We'd have a nice lunch often featuring fresh fish just caught and cleaned. Sometimes, Earl and Jewell, and cousin Richard would be camped there, and we'd have a big time and lunch together. In the summers we often camped there a couple of days at a time. Sadly, for me at least, siltation finally cut off this big cove and now it is an isolated back-water. I don't go there anymore.

 ## 35 SUMMER OF THE BIG STRIPERS

On July 2, 1981, Dad and I put the boat in at Burn's Run. As usual we arrived at the gate about 5:45 a.m., and, as usual, had to wait until the 6 a.m. opening. After launching the boat, we still had to wait for daylight in order to start hunting the fish. We spent the time tying on lures and eating a sausage biscuit breakfast washed down with steaming coffee from the thermos.

The morning was bright, still, and warm; the night's low temperature had been about 78 in keeping with the 100 + temperatures we'd been having in the daytime. Even though the days had been hot and still, the fishing had been fabulous for stripers in the 4 lb to 7 lb class. We were anticipating another day of good top-water fishing. We each, as was our custom, brought two rods—they were medium-heavy power with Ambassadeur casting reels loaded with 14 lb Trilene line. Our lures were reliable top-waters—a pencil popper on one rod and a smaller pico-pop on the other. My favorite pencil popper was a chrome-sided blue-backed job. Dad's was a shad-colored one called Smoky Joe. We each used a silver-colored pico-pop and white bucktail on the second rod. The reason for using a big lure, the pencil popper on one and a smaller lure, the pico-pop on the other, was determined strictly by the preferences of the fish we were after. We'd found that we were more successful if we "matched the hatch," meaning our baits were large if the prey of the fish were large, and small baits were preferred if they were feeding on small fish. However, this morning, the fish weren't doing anything early--unlike previous days when *early* was great!

About 8:30 am, along the dam, near the north end, some big shad began flaring and fleeing. Big fish, in fact, enormous fish began smashing into the shad schools. Shad were jumping in a frenzied attempt to escape the voracious stripers! The water was churning white by enormous fish blasting the shad. We cast our baits into the melee—first the pencil poppers and then the pico-pops. Didn't matter! The stripers tore into our baits with wild abandon. The battles were fierce, no holds barred, the fish were landed and released as soon as possible. Most of the fish were unhurt. We kept only three—the biggest we caught. A couple of smaller four and five pounders were deeply hooked, and we boxed them also. We weighed the three biggest and estimated the smaller ones. Dad had two enormous fish—his largest went 19 lbs. He also had one that weighed 13. Mine was a 13 pounder, and we had caught about 25 others from 4 to 8 lbs. I estimated the total live weight of our morning's catch at about 200 lb, most were safely released!

I'd taken Papa Earl striper fishing a number of times that summer. He'd never lure fished much, had spent his fishing time, many years, trotlining for catfish in the Widow Moore area at the north end of the lake. Of course I'd bragged to him about the Burn's Run trip, and he was ready to go. So on the 27th, he arrived at the house about 5 a.m. Eurith fixed us a good breakfast and then we hit the road.

I used the same tackle as always, same reels and rods as before. Earl had a fine quality Eagle Claw rod and also a True-Temper. They were 5 ½ footers with short handles. This was standard striper tackle for those days. His reels were Zebcos, one was a model 800, the other a, too-light, 33. His line was just 12 lb test. This presented a problem later in the day.

About 8 o'clock we began seeing top-water action along the dam. It was good, and we caught a dozen or so around 4 to 7 pounds. Good practice for Papa Earl! His light line was broken by a rambunctious 5 lb fish and there went a pencil popper. Didn't matter because I'd put 7 of these lures and an equal number of pico-pops in my tackle box. I'd also brought a dozen bucktail jigs in the 3/8 and ½ oz class. We tried those, and they worked fine for smaller fish.

The day grew hot—we were headed for 100 easily. Maybe more! About 10:30 we took a time out for some cold water. We also bathed our faces and necks with ice water and towels. This cooled us down nicely.

I told Earl we'd quit when he wanted. I didn't want the heat to get to him, and we'd already had a good morning He replied that he was OK and would like to fish a little while longer. Presently I heard a fish strike. Nothing sounds just like a big striper blasting a large shad. It is an unmistakable sound! Carefully I searched our surroundings. West of the dam there was, and still is, a large island. I noticed a wave of disturbance off the island's tip. I studied it carefully. Suddenly the water came alive! "Look at that!" I told Earl excitedly. And enormous school of huge stripers was "herding" a bunch of big shad toward the dam. I cranked up the motor, and we moved to intercept the fish and bait. This school of stripers was the biggest I've seen, even till now. The fish were "hogs"—some appearing to be 25 to 30 pounders. One of the biggest struck a shad within a paddle's length of where I was sitting in the back of the boat! We fought fish and fought 'em some more. They were so big that the time consumed by one fight, limited our number of hook-ups. Earl's light line 12 lb test, was easily broken by the monsters. Each break-off meant another pencil-popper good-bye! I didn't care—for the fishing was the thing! Stupendous!!!!!!

This was the conversation as best as I remember: "Papa Earl, why are you casting on the south side of the boat? The fish are mostly on the north side." "Because," he said, "If I cast on the north side I'm losing a plug to these big buggers!" I told him that the loss of the plugs didn't matter, we were after fish, and we'd quit only when our lure supply was gone!

We fought and landed, fought and landed! The school moved north along the dam. The water in this area, surprisingly, is only about 20 feet deep, and the bottom is covered with second-growth brush that was left when evacuation work was finished, but before the lake filled. That brush grew rapidly and is still firmly rooted in the lake bottom. The problem with the brush was that we began hanging enormous stripers that bored straight to the bottom. Try as we might, we couldn't turn these monsters before they had us broken off. I still believe, and always will, that we had several fish of 25 lb or more on, but our 5 ½ foot black-bass rods imply lacked the power to turn 'em.

Finally it ended! The fish were gone. We were out of lures anyway! Seven pencil poppers and five pico-pops had but the dust! But what a day!!! As accurately as I could count, we'd caught almost 70 stripers—most were over 8 pounds. I'd caught one of 17 pounds and another of 13, and still another of 11 lb. Earl's best was 11 pounds, but he'd caught many of 7 to 9 lbs. He said these were the biggest fish ever for him on rod and reel.

Until he died, Papa Earl remembered this trip. In fact, the very last time we drove across the dam, he talked about it. For both of us, the memories were precious.

36 THE DAM AREA

Until I retired from teaching in 1990, a lot of my fishing in the river system was in the big lake. We striper fished in just about every accessible area—and had great success! Sporadically, I'd make week-end trips to the dam if I'd heard that the fishing was good. Before stripers were introduced, sand bass were the main light tackle item with blue-catfish occupying the big fish niche. This was all OK! Sandies are a great, magnificent light tackle species. No doubt about it—many thousands of sandies were harvested each year during their spawning runs. This, of course, involved fish from downstream tributaries, cut-offs and ox-bows. Many of the sandies were lunkers, even crowding four and five pounds.

The introduction of stripers to Texoma gradually had an effect on the sand bass population. Competition with the big predators thinned the ranks of the sandies in the river as well as the lake. There are still sand bass to be had, and they are often quite large but these days are not their glory days in either place.

The best river fishing, in the vicinity of the dam, occurs during spring-time floods. Most years, in the 1990s and early 2000s, saw such floods take place. As a result of the fertility of the Red River system, flood times are times of plenty for the fish and fishermen and also for the fishing-related economics of the area. At the time of this writing, 2011, we are several years without a flood season, and everyone, including the fish, is suffering.

In 1990, heavy spring rains brought the lake around the spillway. The lake level reached 645 feet, and the fishing in the river was awesome. I fished two days from the south bank, just below the bait house area. The tackle I used was light—a 6 foot 10 inch black bass jigging rod with an Ambassadeur 6500C3 reel and 15 pound Big Game line. My lures were 6 inch, one ounce Pencil Poppers.

Some other fishermen, friendly, said to me, "Your tackle is too small, too light, too short." I said, "I'll try it anyway." In two days with this tackle, I caught 45 stripers. All were caught on the Pencil Poppers. Twenty-six of the fish ranged from four to eight pounds, and I kept a limit of two and three pounders each day. The rest, including all the larger ones, were released. That was the best of many good days that summer. One day, fishing closer to the flood gate, I switched over to the 7 inch chrome and blue redfin and had a ball with fish up to 5 lbs.

During the rest of the summer I switched off to the lake often, boat fishing some and wade fishing a lot in the Platter Flats area. Occasionally, I'd make a trip to the river for cat fishing or for extra light spin fishing with crappies jigs. This style of fishing was a "ball." The Corps ran water out for 6 weeks after the flood season, and with my ultra-light and crappie jigs, the variety was amazing. Buffalo and drum from 10 to 15 pounds, crappie, sandies, stripers—all on 1/8 oz crappie jigs.

Interestingly, during the height of the flood, a huge school of mullet from the salt waters of the Gulf appeared at the dam. Most fishermen didn't know what they were. I recognized them easily because I grew up at Yuba, Oklahoma and spent much of my time fishing Red. Many asked me about them, and I told them what they were, that they were good to eat, and good for bait. Finally, they disappeared—back downstream, I guess. As a boy, many times, I witnessed mullet jumping in the river.

Another interesting thing was that I'd missed a few days fishing at the dam, and when I returned to fish, an acquaintance, told me, "That fellow over there caught a 3 ½ foot tarpon yesterday." I talked to the guy he'd pointed out, and he told me that it was true—just like tarpon he'd caught off the north jetty at Port Aransas. Flood times are interesting times!

37 BIG FISH IN THE RIVER

January 27, 1993 was a beautiful winter day. After lunch I told Eurith, "I'm going to try the river for a while." My tackle that day included a Silstar nine foot, medium-heavy spinning rod and a Quantum GW5 reel loaded with fifteen pound Big Game mono. I rigged it with a two ounce, casting float fitted with a five foot, seventeen pound leader. The lure was a 1/8 oz bucktail jig—white with a sky-blue streak on the back and a 4 inch split-tail trailer in yellow chartreuse.

At the dam, I walked down the main stair access, on the Texas side, to the river. The water release was good; both generators were open, and the river looked clean and clear. I worked my way downstream past the second set of stairs with no action. I stopped and visited with a cat-fisherman. He was the only other fisherman at the low riverside, though there were several on the Texas wall. I fished my way to the third and last set of stairs, to the old pilings without getting a touch. I took my tine—trying long casts, short casts, rapid retrieves, slow ones, hard, splashy ones, more subdued ones—nary a strike did I get. I made my way back upstream, past my original starting point. In this area there was more white water, an indication of the large rocks and boulders along that part of the river bottom. "There should be something around those rocks," I said to myself. After about 10 minutes of futility, I moved about 20 yards downstream. I made a good long cast, angling upstream and past the white-water. I worked the casting float sharply, hoping the combination would jar some sort of fish into action. Finally, as the float reached a point straight across from me, I decided to "dead stick" it a little. After moving about 10 feet downstream, my float suddenly shot under the surface, and my line tightened sharply. "Reckon I've hung a rock," I thought. I gave my rod a sharp rap in an attempt to knock it free of the obstruction. The "rock" rapped back—hard and fast! I was into a fish! A very good one!

The battle was joined, the fish used the current well, my rod was sharply bent, and best of all, that lovely noise that striper fishermen absolutely love—my drag was stripping and whining in protest! Downstream we went. The cat-fishermen pulled his tackle out of the way. "Man, you have a big fish," he said excitedly! I pumped and cranked, pumped and cranked. My reel spool was emptying, but the drag was doing its job though protesting mightily!

Finally, the tide of the battle turned. I was about 60 or 70 yards downstream from where the fish had started. We were now in a calmer, quieter water. I pumped and cranked. "Careful, Kelwyn," I told myself. "Don't rush." I was now rapidly gaining line. I cranked and pumped, keeping a good arc in the rod. At last the great fish surrendered. He now lay at my feet in the water's edge. "Great fish!" the cat-fisherman said. I picked the fish up, gathered my tackle and trudged up the stairs to my pick-up. That was the only strike I'd had all day.

On the way home, I stopped at my Dad's place, and we measured the striper at thirty-four inches. Hog-fat, it weighed just a tad over 18 pounds. Not my biggest striper ever, but my largest in several years, and up to that point, my biggest from the river.

The spring of 1993 was a wet one. The lake level gradually encompassed most of my shoreline fishing areas, and the lake, at times, was discolored by mud from the Red and the Washita. I fished other areas from time to time—successfully at Lake Lavon's Pilot Creek arm for sandies, and one trip to Ray Robert's for crappie. But, my heart wasn't in it. My dad died of pneumonia in March, and grief and sadness wiped out my need for fishing.

After a few weeks though, I went back to the river. A steady uninterrupted water release had brought vast numbers of fish from downstream areas. Catfish and stripers were plentiful, and there was good number of hybrid stripers from Pat Mayse' lake downstream from Texoma. I began fishing again—concentrating for a while on light tackle and small jigs. By the first of May the lake level had jumped to 636 feet, and the flood gates were opened. Big stripers moved in, and the Oklahoma side of the river was hot!

My Quantum GW5 spinning reel had given it up—the anti-reverse suddenly "exploded" in a battle with a good fish, a 7 pounder, and the gears stripped some cogs. So I bought a new reel—a Penn 650SS. At that time, Penn reels were considered the "Cadillac" of spinners, and so, were expensive. Built, quality-wise, they were like a rock—sturdy, smooth, and almost un-destructible. After 18 years, I still have this one, and it has never failed, though it's had some tough duty. I loaded it with 20 lb Big Game, fastened it to the 9 foot Silstar and was ready for action.

Usually, even flood water, when released is clear. But, this time, it was pretty murky, even to the point of being muddy. I gave some thought to the lures I should try during this flood season. I felt that bucktail jigs might be the answer. Their single hook should make them less likely to hang on rocks and their festoons of broken, discarded fishing line. Good sized jigs would cast easily and their thick dressing of hair would slow their fall, especially in the swift water. If a jig did snag up, the single hook should be easier to free than a multi-hooked plug. They would also be much easier to remove from a hooked fish because of the single hook. Such jigs could be made more attractive to the stripers by using trailers—either soft plastic "wiggle tails" or thin pork-rind strips. I'd long been a fan of jigs and had used both bucktail and marabou feather jigs with or without a float when light tackle fishing.

I went to Dave's Ski and Tackle. He's always had an excellent assortment of striper tackle, and he had a good supply of bucktails. I bought a card of a dozen chartreuse 1 oz jigs, and then added another card of yellow ones. Each jig had a $1.29 tag, and I felt that even if I lost a whole card's worth, the cost would still be less than some of the hard plugs in use. I added a couple of packets of trailers—larger than the split tails I ordinarily used with smaller jigs under a float.

At home I rigged a few jigs of each color, placed them along with one Pencil Popper and one Red-Fin in my bag. I then added a pair of long-nosed pliers, and I was ready for action. I decided to start with a yellow-cocktail with an off-white trailer. Using an improved clinch knot, I tied the jig on my line—no snap, no swivel. I was ready! As an after-thought, I added a bag of chartreuse sassy-shad the same size. I also added plain bare jig-heads from ¾ to 1 ½ oz to fish 'em with.

On May 20th I arrived at the river about 7 a.m. I fished only an hour because I quickly had 3 keepers to 7 pounds. Took 'em and cleaned 'em. The chartreuse sassy's on 1 oz headers did the job—better than the bucktails this day. At home, I cleaned the fish while Eurith fixed breakfast. Afterwards I went back to the river.

That morning, I'd maneuvered carefully down the rocks to the water's edge at the flood gate mouth. My technique had been to cast straight out across the released water, let the jig drift down until the line straightened, then reel it in. This was basically a "dead sticking" method. The jig would be carried by the current and seldom would sink enough to snag. This method worked well that morning, but when I returned at 11 o'clock, the place was crowded. I'd lost my spot. I moved down-stream a short distance to a small point where a couple of willow-sprouts grew. I used my pocket knife to trim the willows back in order to have casting room. Now, I could cast back towards the flood gate, and the current would carry the jig toward me.

After a cast or two, I decided to switch from the sassy-shad to a one-oz bucktail and trailer. I found that it was necessary to begin reeling as soon as the jig hit the water. If I didn't, the free-falling jig would be into the rocks and lost. Also, rapid reeling would allow me to keep enough slack out of the line, so that I could observe any twitches resulting from a fish attacking it. I also became aware of an enormous eddy moving upstream along the bank and knowing this, tried to work the jig into the rip between the downstream current and this eddy which was moving in the opposite direction. After a few casts and one lost bucktail resulting from a hang-up, I had the technique down pretty well and could concentrate on my fishing. On about the 5th cast, as I was concentrating on keeping slack from my line, I saw a slight twitch in the line. I quickly jerked the rod tip and, voila, was into a fish! And quite a fish it was. It tore past me downstream, was taking line as it went, and was helped immeasurably by the heavy current. About 50 yards downstream was a small rock point. The swiftest part of the current approached within a few feet of the shore at this point, so I tightened my reel drag as much as I dared fearing a line breakage. But I had to stop the fish! I cranked and pumped and kept the rod in a good arc as well as I could. This combination of things finally began to take toll on the fish. I literally ran to the point. Well, maybe lurched is a better term. Regardless, I had slowed the fish's downstream progress. I finally, by tightening the reel drag, was able to manhandle or force the fish to the rocks, and then, with my gloved right hand, was able to lift him onto the rocks. This was a huge fish, though not quite as big as the eighteen-pounder.

I carried my prize back to my starting point., After putting the fish in my 5 gallon bucket, I was exhausted, but I had to try it again. First cast, worked just as before, and again, I was into a big one! The headlong, mad-scrambling, rock sliding trip to the point, then I landed a twin to the first one. I was TP (totally pooped!)

Returning to my spot, I couldn't resist making another cast. I *should* have resisted and rested a couple of minutes, and certainly should have retied my jig. For the third time, it happened again! But this time was different. The power of the fish along with the power of the current was virtually irresistible. This was not a huge fish—it was absolutely enormous! My rod was doubled over, past the stiff butt section and into the handle. I'd never felt a striper like this one! He headed toward the center of the river. I stumbled, staggered, slid and almost fell a couple of times! Like a boxer on the ropes, a victim of too many Joe Louis punches, but I managed to hang on! Finally, finally I turned him, worked him toward the rocks. He fought dirty! He tried to rub the line between rocks, wallowed, kicked gallons of water with his tail which I could now see was twice as broad as my open, widespread hand, and just as I reached for that enormous head, gave a last ditch jerk of that head and popped that 20 pound line—the line that I had not cut back and retied!

I've always felt that this was the strongest and largest of the thousands of stripers I've met....but this time, THE FISH WON!

The other two that I'd beaten were fat, thirty-two inches, and one was 14 lb while the other a half-pound heavier.

 ## 38 JUNE 1993

Late spring of 1993 was, indeed, a fantastic season of big fish. My nephew, Eddie, and I along with a friend, Dana, took an air-boat trip with a young guide I'd known for years, E.D. Dollar.

E.D. had obviously put in a lot of work and time in prepping for the trip. This was for a half-day of live boat fishing. We all were eager to go, and so met E.D. at the sandy beach landing right there at the dam. Our tackle consisted of 7 foot casting rods, whippy in order to lob the live bait, and Ambassadeur reels loaded with 20 lb line. Ambassadeurs are still favored by most guides because of their castability, line capacity, and durability. They are terrific striper reels! Each rod had a 3/0 Octopus hook tied on and either no weight, or a very light split shot sinker. Basically, we'd free-line live shad.

E.D. slid his air-boat into the water at the Oklahoma sandbar, and we headed for the cable to which we'd tie. Flood water was pouring out the flood gate, and so we circled below the outpour rather than trying to force our way through the raging current.

At that time, June of 1993, the tie-up cable extended to the end of the central wall separating the flood gate from the generators, which were open also. So we were in the midst of a torrent of moving water! The whole thing was quite interesting—big stripers were patrolling the crease between the flood gate maelstrom and the somewhat calmer generator water. In addition, the fishermen upon the Texas wall were hurling epithets as well as Pencil Poppers at the boat, the wall, and the big stripers. But only the Pencil Poppers bothered us—they had hooks!

E.D. had collected gizzard shad early that morning. They were beautiful baitfish—some probably weighed close to a pound. We hooked them through the nose and tried to softly let them into the crease when the majority of the big stripers seemed to be. E.D. made the first cast for each of us, watched us, and decided that we could handle it. He became the man with the gaff.

Huge stripers attacked our baits voraciously. The strikes were fierce, explosive and, when a fish was hooked, the battle was amazingly tough for our relatively limber rods which bent double. The reel drags had to be set just right because if a setting was too tight the line would break on hook dislodge, and if too loose, the fish would go wherever it wanted which was usually in the rocks.

This was an astounding morning of fishing. We boxed 14 stripers which averaged 16 pounds each. Smaller fish, 4-8 pounders, were released. My 5 keepers totaled 96 pounds and included two over 20 pounds. Eddie and Dana had similar results, and Dana, so stressed out by the excitement suffered chest pains. Later, at the Wilson-Jones Hospital emergency room, he was told he'd had a mild heart flare-up!

Later in June, bass fishing with bucktail jigs yielded several more big ones for me in the 10 to 13 pound range. Perhaps 1993 was an unusual year for big flood-time fish, but more often than not, if conditions are favorable, the fishing could be unforgettable.

39 SHORE FISHING

The morning was windless at one of Texoma's rock points. The only evidence of activity was the dimpling of the surface by countless shad. No predator activity was evident. As is customary with my fishing, I'd arrived just before daybreak hoping to at least duplicate what I'd accomplished a couple of days ago—25 to 30 good pan-sized stripers and sandies, all of which had been released. I was using light tackle—a 7 foot Shimano medium spinning rod and an ancient, but reliable Quantum reel loaded with 20 lb braid and a 2 foot leader of Big Game mono. My lure was a simple bucktail jig—with a flat head and a dressing of white and chartreuse hair with no plastic trailer. I've found that this "butterbean" jig can be deadly on small to medium stripers and sandies if used with the proper retrieve. On this trip though, "whipping the butterbean" didn't work. I tried a variety of methods ranging from virtually dead-sticking to extra- speedy. Finally, after good strike, I landed a fat sixteen inch largemouth. But, that was all I could manage with the 3/8 oz jig. I switched off to a yellow jig tied onto a smaller ¼ oz head. On past trips, this lure had worked very well. But, the yellow jig didn't do it either, and I changed lures again to a silver Kastmaster spoon with a single hook and a yellow bucktail tag I'd attached. The ¼ oz metal lure has an enticing wiggle and often works when others won't'.

The first few casts drew a blank, and I was about ready to try another spot when a savage strike on the Kastmaster quickly revived my interest. The fish made a sizzling run straight south and, thankfully, stayed in open water rather than making a left turn and hanging me up on one of the abundant rocks. My light rod was well bent, the fish was obviously a huge one for my light tackle. But, the drag on the old reel did its job in fine fashion! The fish just kept going. Suddenly to my right an explosion of vicious strikes split the surface of the water as a pod of huge stripers blasted into a school of 4 to 5 inch gizzard shad. And here I was, still fighting my hooked fish with a "blitz" going on around me! One of my friends was searching for sandies nearby with a cork and jig. A huge striper smashed his red and white cork; another hit the jig so hard that his leader popped. My friend just reeled in the remnants of his tackle and sat there unbelieving!

At last, after around 10 minutes of pumping and cranking, I had my fish coming my way. Finally, he was at my feet—a beautiful striper which I measured at 31 inches. I seldom weigh large fish any more feeling that the physical stress on the fish is likely to cause a fatal injury. Instead I carefully measure the length of the fish, and noting the fish's physical condition, I refer to a chart which accurately indicates the approximant weight. This is good enough for me and allows for a quick and healthy release of big fish. This one was in excellent condition, and I estimated a probable weight of 12 pounds or so. After sending the striper on his way, I picked up my outfit which was a little more suitable for fighting the big ones—a 10 foot rod, larger reel with 30 pound braid and a 20 lb mono leader. The lure was a "loaded" six inch Pencil Popper. I was ready for the next one!

The pod of big fish was still roaming the point and explosive strikes into the bait school betrayed their presence. I worked the Pencil hoping to get another. Finally, an interest in the plug with a smashing strike! But no contact. I stayed with it though, and the loaded Pencil swayed its tail seductively—and that paid off! Another good fish! But alas, not to be mine! He'd pulled off! Additional casts drew blanks and it was obvious that the school had left the point.

This trip occurred in early September of 2009 and is fairly typical of the shore fishing trips I make. I don't always catch 12 pounders; to the contrary, most of my fish are stripers ranging from around 13 to 25 inches, but there are enough bigger ones to satisfy.

I seldom boat fish anymore—age and other factors have made me realize that there are simpler more comfortable was of fishing that can be just as productive! Over the years I've developed techniques and tackle styles that fit my way of fishing. To me, shore fishing is **not** just bank fishing. It can mean wading or fishing from piers and jetties. It involves covering the water and using the type of tackle which is productive. A good shore fisherman is constantly in a learning mode. He watches and observes carefully the behavior of baitfish, birds that feed on the bait, fish patterns of behavior, and weather conditions particularly with respect to wind and rain. In rivers, he carefully studies patterns of currents looking for rips or seams indicating structures and then tries to match his tackle and techniques to these factors.

Shore fishing from the bank, from a jetty, or wade fishing has several advantages, and one of these is avoidance of the physical hassle (sometimes mental also) that boats entail. For those of us who simply can't afford a good boat or fuel, fishing from shore is a logical and often good alternative. Of course, a major disadvantage is that the fisherman is confined to a much smaller area of the lake, stream or ocean. Therefore, the shore-bound fisherman must be on his toes, be alert and aware of factors which can influence his success, and be able to adjust to situations that arise. Many times weather conditions make a boat trip virtually impossible. High winds, rain shower, or combinations of these factors are examples.

But these same conditions often cause the predator fish to turn on—Big Time! Most of my outstanding fishing trips have occurred when weather conditions are, to put it mildly, "tough!" To sit at home because the day is a windy one is a mistake... Go fishing instead! If at all possible, fish with the wind in your face. Stripers, sandies, and black bass often engage in voracious feeding in such rough weather. Winds tend to push baitfish toward a bank and concentrate them. The predators often feed in a frenzy in such conditions. This constitutes a "blitz," and is one of the things the veteran shore fisherman is constantly looking and hoping for.

My style of fishing utilizes artificial lures, almost exclusively, at present. However, most of the tips I'm about to give are applicable to the bait fisherman too.

There's nothing wrong with bait fishing or fisherman. I've done my share of bait fishing in the past. I've found that I enjoy using lures **more** than using bait. It's that simple. People differ in their approaches to life's activities. As long as it hurts no one, and is legal there is no moral difference–bait versus lures!

Often in the warmer months, it seems best to go early. Fish seem to be more active, at times, around daybreak or shortly before. Some of my best trips have occurred at night. Early trips during the spring though fall months have the added bonus of observing wildlife such as deer, coyotes, raccoons, and others. This is part of nature's splendor and means a lot to me.

Often and unexpectedly though, stripers and sandies will be very active at mid-morning or even midday. Some of my very best trips have involved "blitzes" at such times! Hot spells of feeding activity may often take place late in the afternoon as well! Good tackle is better than junk rods and reels. It functions better, is more durable and is less trouble to deal with. The shore fisherman and the boat fisherman should master the use of whatever tackle he chooses. Back yard practice is OK. Practice at the lake shore is better! A versatile fisherman learns to use a variety of tackle. The capability of using spinning tackle, a fly-rod and a good bait casting outfit often enhances the fishing experience.

For me the very best day for striper activity along the shore, in the fall or winter, is one which is cloudy, maybe chilly, perhaps threatening to rain, and is, generally, unpleasant for the non-fisherman. I've had many top-notch trips when weather conditions were like this. My largest lake striper, a 22 pounder, came on such a day in November. Many other times I've had terrific trips on similar days. Often in such weather, I never even see boat fishermen. On trips I take in late winter or early spring, I go early very often. A couple of hours before daylight is an excellent time to be there! I like to begin the day's fishing by using a medium heavy spinning reel with an 8 foot rod, 30 pound braided line and a two-foot leader of 20 pound monofilament. My lure generally will be a 5 or 6 inch Sassy Shad or a ¾ or 1 oz jig head. My jig preference is the owner bullet head which has a good-sized, heavy hook. This jig-head is perfect for such a large plastic shad.

The most preferable spot, I believe, is a long sloping point with fairly deep water alongside. I make a long cast, usually let it hit bottom, and work it in at a speed which helps me feel the thump-thump of the lure's tail action. I've caught many heavy fish by this method, and I consider this technique to be very reliable. The tackle I use for this is not expensive—a moderately large Quantum reel, 8 foot Eagle Claw rod, and 30 lb Power Pro-line. Obviously, many fishermen choose other brands just as good. This, however, works for me.

Chilly, cloudy, winter days with a brisk north breeze call for walking the bank along a steep point. Some of the year's best fish are likely to be caught at this time. A light bait-casting rod about 7 feet, and a smooth-working, level-wind reel with 14 to 17 pound mono make a nice combo for this style of fishing. One has no need to make long casts since large stripers are often within a few yards of the bank. My favorite lures for this type of situation are four inh Wild-Eye shad in pearl or shad gray, four inch cockahoe minnows, and Sassy Shad in glow-color paired with ½ or ¾ oz jig-heads.

Often, the presence of bait and fish may be indicated by gulls striking the water after food, just as stripers and sandies do. The fisherman can determine a pattern of feeding action and usually take advantage of it consistently for several days. Then like most patterns in nature, things change and new ones emerge. Versatility is a big key to success for the shore fisherman. He needs to notice these pattern changes and adapt to them. Example: A heavy spawn of ghost minnows can fill the shoreline with a rich food source. Stripers and sandies love to feed on these tremendously abundant, but individually tiny, forage fish. Quite often the predators will absolutely refuse to hit lures which are much larger than the forage. Then it becomes necessary to "match the hatch" in size in order to succeed. This may be accomplished by switching, for example, from a 4 inch Wild-Eye to a 1 ½ malabou or bucktail jig, or to try flies such a #4 or #6 clousers. The delivery of such tiny lures to the strike zone can be accomplished in a variety of ways. Tiny jigs, marabou or bucktail, can be freely cast with ultra-light spinning tackle. A 6 to 6 ½ foot rod, whippy and light, matched to a small spinning reel is a delight to use with such small lures. Line can be 4 to 6 pound mono or perhaps 10 pound Power-Pro braid. This light spectra braid is about the same diameter as 2 pound mono, is much stronger, and more sensitive due to its lack of stretch and can be cast much farther. I prefer to tie a short leader of monofilament or fluorocarbon to the Power-Pro, thereby decreasing the visibility of the braid to the fish. The fisherman can use whatever leader length seems to work best for the conditions, although, generally, in my experience, a leader of a foot or so is sufficient.

PART 4: THE GULF COAST

40 THE ARANSAS JETTIES—A MIXED BAG

In late July of 1968 we made one of our frequent treks from Dallas to Port Aransas. "We" included my wife, Eurith, daughter, Sherri, son, Jon, my sister and my dad. Our intention this trip was to stay only a week since we were still emotionally distraught due to the loss of my mother to cancer earlier that year. This trip was tough to make. Mom had enjoyed the coast so much and for so many years. But life goes on and the sharpness of grief, though never disappearing is dulled over time. On Wednesday, our first fishing day, Dad and I caught the jetty boat early for the 6 a.m. run across the ship channel to the north jetty. We'd heard that a good run of big Spanish mackerel was underway and that a scattered variety of other species was available. Dad was armed with a whippy fiberglass rod he'd had custom made several years earlier, and I carried a light Shakespeare Gulf Coast popping rod—a new prized acquisition. Our rods were each 7 ½ footers which was light tackle but still beefy enough to handle a good-sized fish. We had each mounted an Ambassadeur 6000 with 20 lb mono on the rods. In addition, for lure fishing, I carried a light action 7 foot Heddon spinner with a Mitchell 300 and 10 lb live. My lures included short plastic worms of two colors, amber with yellow spots and glow-white rigged on plain ¼ oz jig heads. My shoulder bag also included two 52M mirrolures— numbers 18 and 28. We had rigged our bait casters with popping corks, clinch-on sinkers, and wire leaders about 1 ½ feet in length. The leaders had, at one end, a black swivel and at the other end, a gold 3/0 Eagle Claw hook. The swivel and hook were tied with a haywire twist to the coffee-colored leader material. We'd purchased a quart of live shrimp at Woody's just before stepping on the jetty boat. We were ready for action!

We walked down the jetty from the boat dock toward the surf line. It was evident from the current in the ship channel that the tide was rushing in, there was only a very light southeast breeze. Thanks to these light winds, the water was a beautiful clear blue. Dad remarked, "There should be some action before long."

We stepped off the jetty onto a flat-topped granite boulder placed adjacent as part of the apron. Baiting up we hooked the shrimp lightly under the horn. This would allow the bait to stay lively for a while. Hopefully a predator, either a trout, red or big mackerel, would soon grab the tempting morsel.

Piggy perch and pinfish wasted no time finding our baits and pestered us constantly. We realized that as long as these critters were around there were few predators about.

We changed locations after a while, hoping to find some game fish and escape the fiendish appetites of the trash fish. I tied an amber worm jig onto my spinning line, thereby retiring my bait-fishing outfit so as to avoid feeding all my shrimp to the pests. I began casting into the blue water and worked the jig at a variety of depths and speeds. After a few casts and fruitless retrieves at intermediate depths, I decided to try working the bottom more slowly.

On the second or third cast as I worked the jig, I felt a slight "tick" at my line. I set the hook and after a spirited battle landed a one and a half pound sand trout. Though not exactly what I wanted (a red or speck), I was pleased with this fat sandie. Into the ice chest he went and I proceeded to land a half-dozen more before the school moved off. "Not a bad start," I said to Dad who was still fishing the live shrimp rig. The pestiferous perches (pins and piggies) had moved away, and little activity occurred for a few minutes.

Growing weary of slow-fishing the bottom without results, I sped up my jig retrieve near the surface. Suddenly I had a wicked heavy hit, and, just as suddenly, the fish was gone.

"I've got a good one!" Dad exclaimed. I retrieved my now lureless line, laid the light spinner down and prepared to net his fish. After a drag-pulling, rod-bending, spirited, but fairly short fight, I netted his fish—a beautiful 24-inch Spanish mackerel. :"One of these clipped my jig off," I exclaimed as I cut the tail of the mack to bleed it out before placing it on ice. We fished <u>seriously</u> for the mackerel for about another hour and a half before the tide began to slacken and the fish moved off. Our mackerel battles were hard-fought, entertaining and productive. Finally the fish were gone, as was our bait, and we loaded up our gear and hustled to the dock to catch the jetty boat back across the channel to Mustang Island.

Later at the Angler's Court's fish cleaning house we counted 18 big macks. These were the biggest we'd caught in years as most were in the 24 inch to 28 inch range but one monster was an almost unbelievable 32 inches 7 ½ lb. on the deliar! We planned a return trip to the jetty the next morning.

Fillets from these fish which had been properly bled-out and iced were delicious fried, broiled or however fixed.

The next morning we purchased a quart of bait for each lureset and caught the first jetty boat run. We were confident that we'd have a repeat performance of the previous day's success. To my live bag I'd added several ¾ oz Sprite spoons in both silver and gold. I'd work these with the heavier popping rod rather than the light spinner.

We began fishing at about the same location as where we finished up the day before. Weather and tide conditions were similar though the southeast breeze was a little stiffer.

Action began early and was fast. We each landed several 22 to 24 inch Spanish quickly and it appeared that another great day was shaping up. Suddenly, for some reason the Spanish left and the action came to a halt, but only briefly! Dad had a vicious hit, a terrific fight from a much heavier fish, but he lost the critter as a result of his line being cut above the wire leader. We redid our rigging using longer leaders.

We were back in the game—a school of veracious black-tip sharks had moved in and the battle was on! The fights were terrific with many cut-offs and pull-outs. Each black-tip was released as carefully as possible to avoid killing the fish we weren't keeping and to avoid losing fingers to the wicked teeth of the critters.

At intervals we'd each stop to re-rig or have a drink or just sit on a rock. This kind of fishing is hard work! The school stayed around for a couple of hours. The sharks had apparently trapped a big school of large mullet and mackerel in the "pocket" of the jetty and were voraciously feeding. Their victims were terrified, jumping and attempting to flee the scene. There were numerous explosive strikes as additional predators made their presence known. We felt some of these may have been large jack fish or tarpon, but the black-tips were the only fish we were certain of identity.

The frenzy finally slowed then completely stopped. Two exhausted fisherman then gathered up their somewhat battered gear and made their way to the boat dock. Aboard the jetty boat we talked about the morning's fishing. We estimated that between the two of us we'd fought 12 to 15 of the black-tips, but only pulled 5 on the jetty. These were cut loose and pushed back into the surf unharmed. We killed none. We didn't take time to try to weigh any, but we estimated them to be 15-25 lb. They were very difficult to handle even after hitting the jetty. Our landing net was in tatters, our hands were cut and bleeding from dealing with wire leaders, which incidentally we'd lengthened to about 3 feet to avoid cut-offs from the sharks tails, and we were two of the tiredest, but happiest fishermen around.

 ## 41 A REDFISH FISHING TRIP

I'd heard that the Island Queen a converted ferry boat, was doing well on night time trips to the end of t the Port Aransas jetties in Port Aransas, Texas. Word was that the party boat fishermen were catching black-tip sharks and lots of big redfish with most of the reds being oversized or outside the slot limit. Most fishermen these days seldom kill an outsized red, though legally they may if the fish is properly tagged. Though smaller reds up to ten pounds or so are delicious, the big ones aren't desirable as food since their flesh is tough, bloody, and strong-tasting.

These big ones, known as "bull reds," even though they are females, will typically range from thirty-five inches to forty-five inches, and in weight from fifteen pounds to thirty-five pounds. They are terrific fighters, and the catch and release fishery for these big mams is great fun.

Our trip to the coast in October of 2003 had not been productive for fishing, though we'd certainly enjoyed our stay on the island. My wife, Eurith, suggested we try the party boat. We'd fished on the Island Queen many times and found the trips, almost without exception, to be enjoyable and productive.

We bought our tickets at Woody's for the six pm to ten pm trip to the end of the north jetty. We were told that about twenty-five fishermen would be aboard.

Most of the passengers used the boat's tackle, and it was certainly adequate—6 ½ to 7 foot boat rods, good reels with 25 lb line and, for the jetty fishing, 4/0 hooks and bank sinkers. The sinkers were tied to the end of a 30 lb leader with the hook tied about ten inches above the four ounce sinker. Such a heavy weight was needed because the currents were fierce at the jetties when there was tide movement.

I elected to rig our own tackle. We'd found it to be more than adequate on earlier Island Queen trips. Eurith's outfit consisted of a 7 foot medium-heavy Lightning Rod and an Ambassadeur 6500C reel with 25 lb Big

Game line. My rig was an All-Star 6 ft 10 in Jig special, a 6500C and, big mistake, 20 lb thin mono-fine for striper fishing in Lake Texoma, but a disaster waiting to happen on this trip.

The boat, finally, after several tries, was securely anchored just inside the end of the north jetty, about forty yards from the rocks and in about thirty feet of water. Deck hands brought fresh, dead shrimp and cut-bait around to the bait holders. The cut-bait consisted of pinfish and pogies, halved.

The group of fishermen seemed friendly though boisterous. "We may have a bunch of drunks," I muttered to Eurith. "Just fish," she said, "and don't worry about it."

We baited up and, when the deckies gave the word, dropped our baits to the bottom. Hard-head city! These wiggly, spiny, detested little catfish were all over us! Some were 1 ½ pounders, and many were 6 inches. Regardless, a person knew he'd probably get jabbed. The deck hands were busy; actually, they were snowed under with the task of hard-head removal. Of course, I elected to dehook those of my wife and my own, and naturally, I was jabbed, re-jabbbed, and then, once more jabbed for good measure! Blood streamed from my hands. I rubbed slime from the fishes belly on the cuts and somewhat relieved the pain, but Eurith was becoming the hard-head queen of Texas. She kept a steady stream of the wiggly little devils coming over the rail. The crowd was getting into it as well. There was lots of good-natured kidding and laughter. I thought to myself, "Not a bad bunch to be with at all!" As far the fishing went, it began to look like a bum trip — hard-heads or nothing.

Just about dark I put the tail half of a pogie on and sent it to the bottom. After a few seconds I had a solid bump. I didn't have to set the hook; he was on! I was in business — a terrific fight — for about 30 seconds. He went under the boat. I put the rod to him, big time! Everything held, except the thin 20 lb line., I t popped right in two. Examination showed severe abrasion. A combination of barnacles on the boat bottom and thin diameter had done the job. Wonderful co-polymer, thin, supple, highly publicized! A big bust for me. A rare big-fish opportunity wasted.

Angry at myself for trusting the thin line, I decided to rectify the situation. In my tackle bag I had a spool of 25 lb Big Game I'd brought for leaders. I immediately sat down on the bench at our station and began stripping co-polymer from my reel. Eurith kept catching hard-heads. A young blond woman fishing next to us, with her mother, tied into a big one. Down the rail she went, a deckie with a net following. And here I was working on my tackle! The deck-hand landed the blonde's redfish. "Thirty-nine inches," the deckie said after a few moments. "Please put him back," the young lady said.

I stripped line, and stripped more! Eurith was catching hard-heads to beat sixty. Big fish were thumping as they hit the deck. "I can only catch hard-heads," she complained. "Try a bigger bait," I told her as I continued to strip line. She did, and then caught bigger hard-heads.

My fellow fishermen, and the deckies too, thought I was insane crazy! The deck hands looked at me, shook their head and walked off muttering among themselves. People talked. "He's using his own tackle. His hands are bleeding. Disgusting!" I was the goofy guy on this trip. Eurith was still catching hard-heads.

Finally I reached the knot, clipped the co-polymer free, wadded it into a ball; into my pocket it went. Now to tie the Big Game line onto the remaining short length on the spool I couldn't see, it was too dark! My glasses? At the cabin, on the dresser, neatly cased to take fishing! I knew I'd left something behind. Now I remembered what it was. Big fish were now hitting the deck with regularity.

I tried to start a blood knot. I fumbled and fumbled. A fellow at the other end of the boat decked a black-tip shark of about 15 lbs. The blonde's mother offered to help me, but Eurith forsook her hard-head fever and finished the knot for me. She did the job and it worked. Big fish were still coming over the side. Deckies were still coming by, shaking their heads, eyes to the sky, whispering and laughing about the crazy, fat, bearded man working on his tackle when the fishing was so good.

Out of pity, one of the deck hands laid a 4 oz sinker and a hook by me. Eurith and our fishing friends of the evening clucked with sympathy. Racing against time, Eurith held the spool of Big Game on a length of dowel rod, and I speed-reeled, filling my spool. Now I had to do my terminal tackle. Fortunately I could do this by feel and didn't have to see.

Back in business again, finally! Big fish were still coming over, and Eurith still had the monopoly on the hard-heads. The champion of the boat as a matter of fact! Another black tip shark hit the deck—about ten pounds. Reds of 35 inches or more were still pounding the deck. I baited up with the head half of a pogie, dropped it to the bottom, and had a wicked strike. I set the hook. Then I was joined by my lovely wife—hard -head city, big time. Not a red, but, at least a fish.

The pace of big ones coming over the rail slackened. Most were released, but some were tagged and put into the box. I was resigned to my fate. No big ones for me. That was ok because of the tuna trip last week. Rationalization! That's what Dr. Hunziker, of my college days, called it—rationalization! Live with your failures.

My hands were hurting and bloody with hard-head induced wounds, but I had a half-bottle of water. My neighbor asked, "Are you ok?" I nodded, refreshed, and headed back to the rail. Tap, tap, another hard-head? A little different something was chewing on my half-a-bunker. It moved a little so I could feel the weight, then I set the hook. Off to the races we went! The battle was joined! Long-live redfish! Down the rail we went. A deckie cleared the path, and I tried to keep up with the fish while putting on pressure with the stiff rod butt. The deckhand asked, "Do you still have 20 lb line on?" I told him that I now had 25 lb Big Game line on. He beamed with happiness, so he must have thought we had a chance!!!! My light rod, developed for black bass fishing did its job, and the knots held and the drag was smooth.

Finally, my friend, the deckie says, "I have him, it's over!" With the aid of a big landing net, he deposited a huge redfish on the deck. The crowd cheered with a standing ovation! Eurith kissed my cheek while the blonde kissed the other cheek. I was offered a million dollar contract..... well, maybe not!

"He caught it with light tackle, his own," a voice said. "His hands are bleeding." I was now a member of the fraternity, and Eurith, with love in her eyes, checked on my health and hugged me! A huge fish 39 ½ inches and weighing 20 pounds, if an ounce.

Back to the sea for that redfish, a dear friend of mine by then. We had competed, and we'd fought. We respected each other completely and were combatants no longer; we had promised not to devour one another.

Eurith was now the hard-head queen of Texas with at least 30 of those spiny devils. I only had a paltry dozen, but had ONE BIG REDFISH! A beautiful night and a wonderful party with a boatload of beautiful people!

PART 5: FISHERMAN WISDOM

42 WORD OF ADVICE

In using spinning reels, learn to close the bail manually—this will prolong the life of the bail springs and will also help prevent line twists. With braid or spectra, before closing the bail after a cast, lift and seat the line on the spool. Practice this often and it will soon become second nature.

Learn to watch for signs of fish-feeding action. This may appear as flashes and swirls of feeders. Birds diving to the water surface, the appearance of "bait slicks", and skittering bait are possible clues to feeding action. In rivers, boils and rips which appear are indicators of underwater structures such as boulder which would furnish a break from swift water. Bait and predators are both likely to occur in such areas. Learn to use your tackle as efficiently as possible. Develop an ability, to tie useful knots reliably, and most of all, be observant toward what is happening in the water.

43 IRREVERSIBLE CHANGES

The river and the lake have changed a great deal down through the years. This is, of course, predictable in light of man's environmental modifications. Some of the changes are unavoidable.

One of the biggest problems is siltation. The surface acreage of the lake, usually listed in literature as about 95,000 acres, is considerably less than it was in the beginning. A smaller lake fills faster, empties faster, cools off sooner, heats up sooner, is more readily filled with silt, and shows effects of pollution by all sources in prominent ways. Developments in real estate with sewage output, lawn fertilizers, and just plain junk hasten the demise of once beautiful, healthy, productive lakes. Texoma and Red River are no exception to these changes, and have had great ecological systems—for people, for nature—including fish, wildlife, and the area's economy. They deserve our protection, not our pollution.

Other changes include the zebra mussels which have invaded the lake and river system, and potentially, may be a serious problem primarily because of their harm to boats, marinas, and the electric generators. Being plankton filter feeders, the mussels may ultimately damage the fishery.

The lake also has a large population of small mud crabs, but this is probably a good thing since they are another food source for all the predators from sunfish to blue-catfish.

EPILOGUE

As I write this in early December of 2011, it occurs to me that I'm now, indeed, an "old man" of fishing. Lots of "water under the bridge" since my first recalled fishing trip on a soft spring day in 1938. Dad, Mom, my grandparents and baby sister drove to Eagle Lake at Karma in the model A.

I remember granddad cutting me a willow pole, equipping it with hook, line a sinker and a cork floater. The bait was red worms from a Prince Albert can. The fish were bream of multi-colored various species, and I must have caught half a hundred of 'em. Since that trip I've been "hooked" on fishing.

I've tested the clear, virginal waters of Glover, Mountain Fork, and Little River, and been rewarded with countless hours of delight in the fishing and the joy of camping with my loved ones—uncles, aunts, cousins, and, later, my precious Eurith and our kids. These memories are the jewels of my life. I'll never forget them as long as I have sense.

Fishing has taken me to the Texas Coast, to assorted lakes in streams of Texas and Oklahoma, to oxbows and beautiful creeks of Arkansas, and to many delightful wetlands and ponds of this area. I've been very fortunate to have good health and the patience of my loving and lovely wife during these years.

Many changes have taken place in the landscape over the years—mostly to the detriment of the natural environment. I'm saddened because there are generations now who will never see the beauties of nature that I remember.

I thank my loved ones, including God Almighty, for allowing me those times!

Kelwyn Ellis

APPENDIX: LEADERS, KNOTS, AND RIGS

Attaching a leader to the main line can be a problem. I've found that an excellent knot of this is a triple Surgeon's (Surgeon's Knot | Killroy's Fly Tying, 2012). It is fast and easy to tie, and, if done properly, is a 100% knot.

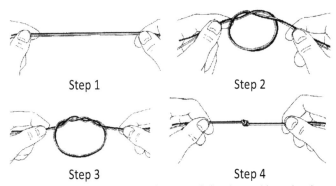

Step 1   Step 2

Step 3   Step 4

To tie this knot, cut a piece of mono of the desired length, plus several inches, from the spool. Example: If I want a two foot mono leader, I'll cut a piece of Big Game mono of about 30 inches from a bulk spool. Lay the piece of mono alongside the end of the spectra running line. Overlap the ends of the two about 6 to 10 inches. Hold the ends of the line together and tie them with a simple overhand knot. Do **not** pull the overhand knot shut, but leave an open loop. Repeat the process-run the ends of the two lines through this open loop. This now double overhand knot constitutes a single surgeon's knot. Do not stop now because it is weak, but repeat until the ends of the leader and the running line have been brought through the loop a total of six times. As the knot is tied, the lines become stiffer and the knot more difficult. An aid such a pencil or a small screwdriver can be used to pull the ends of the two lines thought the loop. Once there, six overhand, loose knots have been produced. You now have a rather messy looking loop. Moisten the whole thing thoroughly. Hold the opposite ends of the lines and firmly, but slowly, pull them together. The loop shrinks, disappears, and presto, you have a beautiful triple surgeon's knot. Remember, each surgeon's knot requires a double overhand, therefore, a triple surgeon's knot necessitates **6** overhands! When finished, snug the tag ends close to the knot. Once mastered, you have a knot which is 100%, is very durable, and any breakage of the leader is more likely to happen along the leaders length than at the knot.

An obvious alternative to the ultra-light spinning tackle is fly-fishing. A 4 or 5 weight rod, approximately 7 ½ to 8 feet long, matched with sparsely tied Clouser minnows such as #4 or #6 that are tied to the leader with a loop knot (Tying Instructions For The Non-Slip Loop Knot, 2012) does the trick.

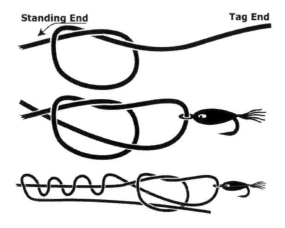

The non-slip loop knot is extremely useful for the attachment of a jig or fly to the end of a lure or leader. Since it does not fit tightly to the lure, the knot allows a bit more action which is more attractive to the fish.

I prefer a simple, single-action, light fly-reel with 50 yards or so of backing. I've found that a variety of fly colors is good—white, blue/white, even blue over chartreuse will catch, but my best results have been obtained with chartreuse over white. Sparsely tied small flies with bead-chain eyes rather than the customary lead ones are best for this situation.

An alternative to the fly rod or ultra-light spinning is the use of a "cork and jig" system. This technique allows the use of heavier tackle and when mastered can yield amazing results. The system I use for "setting up" a cork and jig is thus.

(a) Select a proper sized floater of Styrofoam or balsa wood. Such floaters are available at most tackle shops around our lakes and are also available along the gulf coast. These "corks" may range in weight from ½ oz to 4 oz. By the way, actual cork floaters are seldom used. Those of Styrofoam or balsa seem to work better in this method.

(b) The floater probably is set up with a length of aluminum wire through its center. At the bottom a lead weight is fastened and at the top, usually a bead, probably red in color, and then a loop is bent into the wire to hold the deal together and to fasten the leader.

(c) Place a sturdy split ring on the wire loop

(d) On the split ring, place a swivel. I prefer one in black and, for a 1 oz or 1 ½ oz floater, I generally use a number 7 swivel.

(e) Also place a snap swivel on the loop of the floater. I prefer a quality ball-bearing swivel to help reduce line twist and to reduce "kinking" in your leader.

(f) Note here that everything attaches to the top of the floater. The running line, from the reel, attaches to the swivel on the ring, and the leader attaches to the ball-bearing swivel.

(g) Fasten the running line to the swivel on the split ring, **not** to the snap swivel on the ring. This is for the leader. An easy way to do this is to use either a plain sturdy snap or a snap swivel. A problem to be overcome is the twisting of the floater and leader as the lure is retrieved. Quality swivels, either ball-bearing or plain, will help accomplish this.

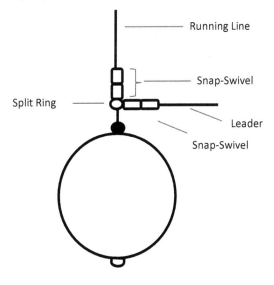

(h) The leader itself may be of whatever the angler desires. I generally use 15 or 20 pound monofilament. Big Game mono is good. It is durable, resistant to fraying, and has excellent knot strength. Fluorocarbon leaders are also excellent. Remember, it has less stretch, and its best strength, I have found, is not quite up to the quality of mono. Leader length is up to the angler. For long-rod fishing, I generally use a 4 ½ to 5 foot leader which works for me. Don't forget that everything attaches to the **top** of the floater. Resist the temptation to tie to the wire of the lead weight at the bottom of the floater. If you tie to the bottom, a pendulum effect will result in tangles, the complexity of which is astounding!

(i) The improved clinch knot (Clinch Knot | Killroy's Fly Tying, 2011) is probably the best for attaching the leader to the cork or to the line.

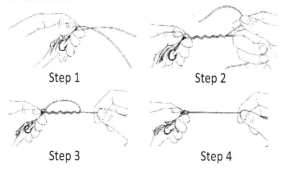

Step 1   Step 2

Step 3   Step 4

Be sure to make 5 turns in doing this knot. I add one more step to "lock" the knot. That is, to run the leader end back through the loop at the lure or swivel, moisten with saliva, and snug it firmly. I use this lock any time I tie the clinch knot. With it in place I've never had a knot open, but before I began using it, occasionally a big fish would be lost. I've lost my share of 'em, but since using the lock step, my losses haven't been from knot failure.

(j) Now for the tackle to use with "float and jig." I've found that a quality spinning outfit seems to work fine for this method. I've also used bait-casting (level-wind) tackle, and it does a decent job if the angler handles it well. The use of spinning tackle seems to me, to be a better method because the shore fisherman is often casting into the wind, which sometimes is near gale force, and usually is trying to reach that surfacing school "way out there." The choice of size of the spinning rig depends upon the conditions and the size of the fish encountered. I'd say that a rod selection, which includes a light 7 footer, a medium 8 or 8 ½ footer, and a heavier 10 to 12 footer gives an excellent assortment when matched to an appropriately size reel. At present my own set of tackle includes the following light tackle rigs:

a.   7 ½ foot medium power rod, #50 sized spinning reel with 15 lb Power-Pro braid, and

b.   8 foot medium power rod, same size reel and line as with the 7 ½ footer

Good brands include St. Croix, Daiwa, Shimano, and Quantum. My heavier setups include:

a.   8 ½ foot and 10 foot medium-heavy power and #60 size reels with 30 pound Power-Pro.

This group of rods and reels is sufficient for most situations where spinning tackle is desired. Remember, game fish, particularly the pelagic ones, do not roam the shore for the convenience of the angler, but are often "out there" a goodly distance. In order to catch 'em, you've got to reach 'em! Heavy, long rods are not the most pleasant to fish with. In an earlier section I mentioned my preference for lighter weight, but I like to use powerful, bait-casting tackle for those times, such as winter, when stripers and other predators are roaming the shoreline. A light-weight outfit such as this can actually tame a heavy fish in a more efficient manner than a longer, heavier one. Example: the 22 pound striper, my largest from the lake, was caught on a 5 ½ foot medium power Fenwick rod and a narrow spool Ambassadeur loaded with 12 pound line. With this relatively small outfit, I was in control from the start, a feeling I've not always had with big fish and spinning tackle!

(k)   Now a word about braided spectra line. I use Power-Pro, but there are many good brands. I use these modern braids only

127

on spinning tackle. The property which makes them desirable to me is their thinness. Example: 30 pound Power-Pro is about the same diameter as 10 pound mono—on the average. It lacks stretch, has a high degree of sensitivity, and is durable. It also can develop "wind-knots" easily, can cut your fingers to the bone and requires knots that are different than those with mono. In addition, it is more visible than mono, and, I believe, for some purpose, requires a leader of mono or fluorocarbon. The wind knots that it develops can be astounding and occasionally impossible to resolve. It is also **expensive**. Then you ask, why use it? Pure and simple, in one word—DISTANCE!

I believe that if one is to become a successful shoreline fisherman, he must learn to properly use a variety of tackle. For me, spinning outfits loaded with spectra-line are the most versatile. But there are basic skills and techniques which, once learned, will make for a happier fisherman.

When loading your reel with spectra, *always* use monofilament backing. Tie the mono to the spool arbor with a reliable knot—I generally use a slip knot and a couple of half hitches. The thin diameter of even heavy-pound test spectra makes it unnecessary to totally fill the spool with it. Once the mono backing is tied, reel the mono to fill the spool to about two-thirds capacity. Now tie the spectra to the mono. I've found the best knot for this is a back-to-back eight-turn uni knot. (Sherry, 2011)

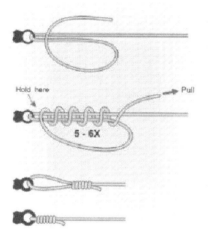

1. Run line through eye of hook or lure and double back parallel to the standing line. Make a loop by laying tag end over the double line.

2. Make 6 turns with the tag end around the double line and through the loop.

3. Moisten lines and pull tag end to snug up the turns.

4. Slide knot down to eye or leave a small loop if desired.

This is strong connection and, if properly tied, will not slip or otherwise open.

Always moisten the knots before pulling tight. Then clip the tag ends close. Mono can be easily snipped with nail clippers, but spectra requires something sharper. I've found that small scissors made by Fiskar do a very adequate job when dealing with spectra. These are available at Wal-Mart or hobby shops such as Michael's. In fishing with spectra line, occasions arise on almost every trip which require that the line be trimmed or cut. For this reason I always have a pair with me in my lure bag.

Many of the knots a fisherman has learned in using mono for years either won't hold with spectra or must be modified in order to be reliable. Blood knots, which are often to join mono to mono, won't work with spectra. The back to back uni knot (already discussed) is fine for use in filling a reel or in tying a mono leader to the spectra running line. I've found that, for tying on a leader, the best knot, however, is a triple surgeon's knot whose directions were given earlier in this chapter.

Why bother, you ask, with a leader? If you are casting a plug or soft plastic bait, inevitably there are hang ups Attempting to break away from such a hang-up is an unpleasant, but common, part of shoreline fishing. A twenty-pound leader is more easily broken than a thirty-pound spectra running line. Always wear gloves when pulling against a spectra hang-up to avoid nasty cuts! Also, at least under certain conditions of water clarity, predators such as black bass, stripers, redfish, and speckled trout, require a short leader because of the visibility of spectra.

A number of other knots should be learned if one intends to obtain the greatest benefit from spectra. These include the uni knot (already discussed), of which there are a variety of uses, and the palomar (Sherry, Palomar Knot - How To Tie a Palomar Knot, 2011) which is excellent for fastening a snap or swivel to the end of a spectra running line.

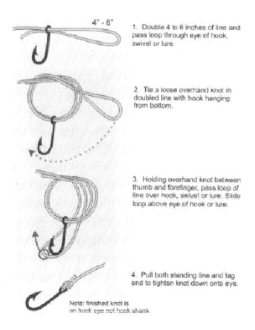

1. Double 4 to 6 inches of line and pass loop through eye of hook, swivel or lure.

2. Tie a loose overhand knot in doubled line with hook hanging from bottom.

3. Holding overhand knot between thumb and forefinger, pass loop of line over hook, swivel or lure. Slide loop above eye of hook or lure.

4. Pull both standing line and tag end to tighten knot down onto eye.

Note: finished knot is on hook eye not hook shank.

These knots, the improved clinch, the non-slip loop, and the surgeon's loop, are also good to use with mono.